Sweater
SURGERY

QUARRY

First published in the United States of America by
Quarry Books, a member of Quayside Publishing Group
100 Cummings Center
Suite 406-L
Beverly, Massachusetts 01915-6101
Telephone: (978) 282-9590
Fax: (978) 283-2742
www.quarrybooks.com

Library of Congress Cataloging-in-Publication Data
Girard, Stefanie.
Sweater surgery: how to make new things from old sweaters/ Stefanie Girard.
p. cm. — (Domestic arts for craft girls)
ISBN 1-59253-420-1
1. Clothing and dress—Remaking. 2. Sweaters. I. Title.
TT550.G57 2008
646.4'04--dc22
2007039104

ISBN-13: 978-1-59253-420-3
ISBN-10: 1-59253-420-1

10 9 8 7 6 5 4 3
Photography: All photography by Lexi Boeger Photography with the exception of pages 134–139 and page 143 courtesy of Armour Sans Anguish
Design: Laura McFadden Design, Inc.
Cover Design: Laura McFadden Design, Inc.
Illustrations: Judy Love
Templates: Stefanie Girard
Technical Editor: Beth Baumgartel

Printed in China

Sweater

SURGERY

how to make new things with old sweaters ~ STEFANIE GIRARD

BEVERLY MASSACHUSETTS

QUARRY BOOKS

Contents

Introduction

Section 1: Getting Started

9   Choosing the Sweater
10 Sweater Construction and Styles
11 Washing and Blocking Sweaters
12 Felting
14 Equipment and Tools

TAKING THE SWEATER APART

16 Types of Sweater Seams
17 When to Cut Seams Apart
17 When to Take Seams Apart
18 Using Existing Design
    Elements and Edges
19 Reclaiming Yarn from
    the Sweater

SEWING THE NEW DESIGN

20 Hand-Sewing Basics
22 Machine-Sewing Basics
22 Construction and
    Decorative Stitches

Section 2: The Projects

28 A Bird in the Hand Purse
30 Gathering-Up-the-Goodies Bag
32 Color-Me-Happy Striped Purse
34 Limelight Purse
36 Pink Pizzazz Purse
38 Cheerleader Purse
40 Merry Mittens & Stocking Set
42 Zap & Shine Pink Felted Mittens
44 Baby's Got the '80s Goin'
    on Booties
47 Toe-Tappin' Booties
48 Pom-pom Hat
50 Scarf of Many Colors
52 Keyhole Scarf
54 Snow White Scarf
56 Peppermint Patti
    Swirl Necklace
58 Green-with-Envy Necklace
60 Jujube Necklace
63 Twiggy Headband
64 Forever-Plaid Skirt
66 Floral Jumper &
    Super-Skinny Belt
69 Green Hoodie
70 Toasty Turtleneck Shrug
72 Pom-pom Sweater
74 Hippie Chicks
76 Woolie Minkie
    & Woolie Piggie
80 Hoot-Toot the Owl
82 Bloomin' Place Mats

84 Nine-to-Five Magazine
    File Cozy
86 Sophisticated Pillow Collection
91 Piles o' Pot Holders

Section 3: Gallery 92

Section 4: Patterns 144

158 Resources
159 Contributors
160 About the Author/
     Acknowledgments

USING SWEATERS AS FABRIC to make something new combines two of my favorite things: the almost instant satisfaction of sewing and my love of knitwear, with its amazing textures, patterns, and fibers. Oh, and let's not forget about the fun of shopping! Treasure hunting in thrift stores for secondhand sweaters often leads to a romp down memory lane or to unexpected and exciting surprises.

Recycling sweaters just makes sense. It's good for the environment, you can't buy sweater fabric, and a lot of us don't always have time to knit something ourselves. And, what better way to preserve a memory than to make something fun or useful from a well-loved sweater that belonged to you, a close friend, or a favorite family member, especially when the sweater is slightly damaged or stained and can't be worn.

Which comes first—the idea for the project or the found sweater? Both! Often, a found sweater is a source of inspiration when you realize, "I know I can make something cool with that!" Alternatively, inspiration may spring from a magazine or from someone walking down the street. Then the hunt for the perfect makeover sweater ensues. With a stash of sweaters,

some basic sewing skills, and the tips and techniques found in this book, you can create unique garments and accessories that are yours and yours alone.

It's a bit of a mind twister to think of sweaters as fabric. Sweaters already have shape, seams, and details. You can incorporate these elements into your designs or remove them and use the sweater as a two-dimensional piece of fabric. Either way, knitted sweaters are full of possibilities.

Like woven fabrics, sweater fabrics stretch and drape in a variety of ways. Different sweaters, or even different areas of the same sweater, may have different weights, weaves, and textures. And as with fabric, these attributes can be manipulated and altered.

Felting is one way to stabilize and thicken a knit made from wool or other animal fibers. This is particularly beneficial when you are making a project that needs to be strong, such as a purse or bag. Stabilizers and backing fabrics are used to minimize or eliminate the stretch of flexible knits. Some stabilizers are used only temporarily, so that the knit is stable during sewing but regains its flexibility once

the stabilizer is removed. Stabilizers and backing fabrics also add weight and body to light-weight sweaters, if the project calls for greater stability. Clever techniques and innovative products have made it much easier to work with "sweater fabric."

When I am shopping for sweaters, fabric, yarn, and trim, the feel is as important as the look. I'm the type of person that "pets" fabric. I have to touch everything! The texture can be in the yarn the sweater is knit from, or in the stitch pattern. It is very exciting to create a dimensional project by manipulating sweaters with bobbles and cables.

The color of the yarns and the weave of the sweater, whether open or closed, are also exciting design elements. For instance, an open-weave lacy sweater has a bold look when it is backed with a high-contrast colored fabric. It is much more subtle with a backing fabric that has a similar color. Intarsia and Fair Isle sweaters provide wonderful, knitted-in colored patterns, great for manipulating into a patterned accessory.

When shopping for sweaters to transform, look closely at these elements and keep them in mind as you plan your project. You might consider buying an extra sweater to test-stitch your idea.

My most important piece of advice is to sketch first! If you are afraid to take scissors to a sweater—remember, the first cut is the hardest! It gets easier every time, and there are always more inexpensive sweaters out there to practice with.

My hope is that you will enjoy the inspiration and new techniques showcased by the projects in this book to make your old or found sweaters into something new and beautiful. I would say it is just about my absolute favorite thing to do—to transform one thing into another. People might ask if you knit your bag or shrug yourself; be prepared to give the answer: "I designed and sewed it from a recycled sweater!"

Share the passion!

Choosing the Sweater

Sweaters come in a plethora of materials, styles, stitches, and construction methods. Some sweaters lend themselves naturally to certain projects, whereas others may work—but will test your patience. Avoid using an old sweater with extensive damage unless your project is much smaller than the sweater, so you can cut around the damaged area. The sweaters shown in this book are meant to inspire you. You don't need, nor will you be able, to find the exact same sweaters. No problem! Choose sweaters with similar body style and knit construction, and you'll be able to make all these projects… and give them your own unique style.

The cardigan

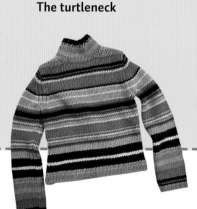

The turtleneck

Sweater Construction and Styles

ANY KNIT SWEATER can be turned into something else, with a little care. A little knowledge about the stitches used to knit sweaters and their various styles will help you choose the most suitable sweater for surgery.

Basic stockinette stitch sweaters are very easy to use and most wool sweaters are made with this stitch. The stitch resembles interlocking V's on one side and interlocking bumps on the reverse side. The garter stitch is also a popular choice. It features the same bumpy texture found on the wrong side of stockinette stitch sweaters on both sides. These two stitches are used in the construction of a large variety of sweaters.

Ribbed stitches are vertical rows of knit and purl stitches. (Knit and purl stitches are the basis for all knitting.) They are very stretchy and typically found at the cuffs, waist, and neck of many sweater styles, although sometimes a whole sweater is knit in a ribbed stitch. Often, the ribbed sections can be incorporated into your new designs.

In addition to the basic stockinette, garter, and ribbed knit stitches, dimensional and decorative stitches are certainly suitable for redesign. Eyelet stitches, lace stitches, other openwork patterns, cable designs, and bobbles generate design interest. Embroidery and embellishment, which is usually added to a sweater after it has been knitted, is fun to incorporate into a new design. It's a quick and easy way to give your project pizzazz.

The openness of the stitching is another design element. Open knits are very flexible and soft, perfect for projects that should drape and flow freely. The open weave also invites you to insert other fibers or ribbon into their holes or to add colorful backing fabric behind the stitches. Closed knits are generally stiffer and, therefore, sturdier. The stitches are smaller, more consistent, and can't be seen through.

Fashion terminology provides a name for most sweater styles. Some of the projects suggest a particular style; others can be cut from any type of sweater. Here is a brief description of popular sweater styles.

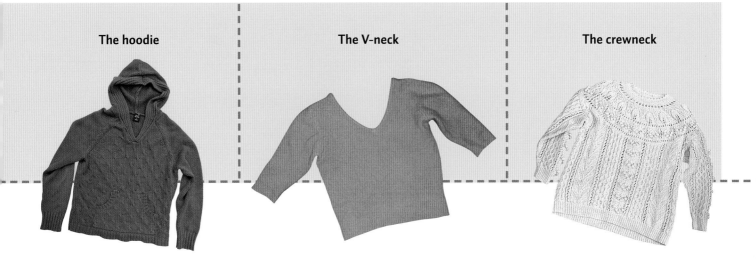

The hoodie   **The V-neck**   **The crewneck**

A **cardigan sweater** is usually collarless and either buttons or zips closed.

A **turtleneck sweater** has a high band collar, which can be folded once or twice to fit around your neck. It is often constructed of a ribbed stitch so that it stretches.

A **hoodie** is a sweater with a hood attached. It can pull over your head or close with buttons or a zipper.

A **V-neck sweater**, as its name implies, has a neckline that is shaped like a V.

A **crew-neck sweater** has a high, round, neckline and it pulls over the head.

A **sweater vest** is a sleeveless sweater that usually pulls over your head, but can also zipper or button closed.

A **raglan sweater** has seams that extend diagonally from the armhole front and back to the neckline (as shown in hoodie above).

A **set-in sleeve** is attached to the body of the sweater in the natural armhole (as shown in cardigan above).

Washing and Blocking Sweaters

Starting with a clean sweater is important. Wash new sweaters to remove sizing and chemicals and wash old sweaters to remove stains and body oils. Since the history of a found sweater is unknown, starting with a fresh, clean sweater hopefully eliminates future surprises. If there is a hole or tear in the sweater, stitch around the opening to prevent its unraveling or getting larger in the washing machine.

Follow the washing instructions on the sweater tag. If the tag is missing, wash the sweater in the washing machine on the gentle cycle with mild detergent. If the sweater loses shape in the washing machine, or if you don't want to put it in the dryer, blocking helps to reshape it. To block a sweater, lay the damp sweater flat on a dry towel, adjusting it until it's the desired shape. Keep it on the towel until it is completely dry. If you are blocking a dimensional project, position it on a similar shaped object instead of a flat towel, so the project dries into the desired shape.

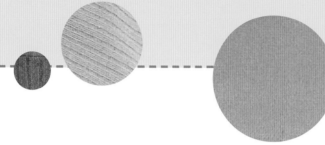

Felting

FELTING IS THE PROCESS of matting and compressing fabric fibers to create a denser cloth. One hundred percent wool sweaters felt the best. Other animal fibers and synthetic fiber combinations work, just not as well. Every fiber felts at a different rate, but it is possible to control the process somewhat.

Wet felting is one of the easiest methods and it cleans the fibers at the same time! It's as simple as throwing the sweater into the washing machine (hot wash water and cold rinse water) with a clean towel and some laundry detergent. The towel helps to agitate the sweater, which facilitates the felting. The longer you keep the sweater in the washing machine, the more the fibers will compress and the stiffer the sweater will be. Check the sweater periodically. If you like the way it looks, take it out and dry it flat on a dry towel (blocking). If you want the sweater to felt more and become smaller and denser, put it in the dryer. You can leave it in until the sweater is partially or completely dry. The sweater stops felting once you remove it from the dryer. You can wash and dry it as many times as you want; each time, it will felt and compress a little more. Don't worry, you can't do anything wrong. Just throw the sweater in the washing machine—you'll be inspired by what comes out!

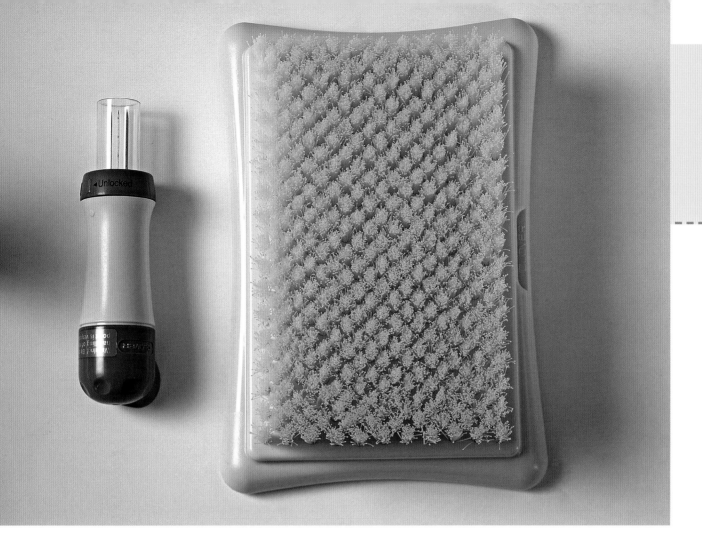

Needle felting is the process of linking wool fabric (or carded or unspun wool) by layering them and poking them with barbed needles. The needles catch and entangle the fibers together. The process is easy, but it takes time and you need to be careful because the needles are very sharp. You'll need a needle-felting tool (or a single handheld needle) and a backing surface. The needle-felting tool has a knoblike handle that holds multiple needles to speed up the process. The backing surface can be a soft, dense piece of foam or a needle-felting mat that resembles a dense brush.

To start the process, determine which fiber (yarn, roving, existing felted sweater fabric) will be the back and which will be the front. Place the back

fiber on the felting mat. Place the top fiber over it and stab it repeatedly with the needle-felting tool, working from the perimeter toward the center. Check the fibers periodically by removing the felting from the work surface. Check that the top and bottom layers are felting evenly and are becoming one new layer. If you want to see only the top fiber from the right side, poke the needle only from front to back. If you want to see both top and bottom fibers on both sides of the felted material, poke from front to back, then flip the layers and poke from back to front. Keep poking until you are happy with your new felted material. You can set the fibers by pressing the back side with a steam iron and a light touch.

Equipment and Tools

Sweater surgery is a breeze with good equipment. You don't need a lot of tools, but the right ones will help turn your visions into reality quickly and easily.

Sewing and Marking Tools

A basic **sewing machine** that sews straight and zigzag stitches and can be adjusted for stitch length, stitch width, and presser foot pressure is perfect. It is also helps to have both a standard presser foot and a zipper foot. Keep a selection of different size **sewing-machine needles** on hand for sewing different fabric weights and thread thicknesses.

Polyester/cotton thread in a range of colors is suitable for most construction sewing. **Thread conditioner/beeswax** tames the thread just as hair conditioner tames hair. It prevents tangling and makes stitching easier.

Straight pins hold knitwear in place and prevent sweater pieces from slipping during stitching. You can also use **water-soluble stay tape or basting tape** to baste or temporarily hold seams together. It makes sewing stretchy knitwear easy.

Safety pins do what they say—they keep you safe from sharp points when you are trying on and fitting your new sweater. Try on anything that requires fitting in front of a **full-length mirror** to ensure that your new fashion statement fits perfectly.

Hand-sewing needles come in many styles. It's a good idea to have a variety on hand. **Sharps** are basic hand-sewing needles. **Embroidery needles** have slightly larger eyes so they can accommodate thicker decorative threads.

Upholstery needles are long, heavy-duty needles that are great for sewing though pillows and cushions. Large-eyed **yarn needles** come in different

sizes and colors for sewing with yarn. If you have trouble seeing the needle as you stitch, try using one that contrasts in color with your project.

Dressmaker's chalk or a **fabric-marking pen** allows you to sketch on your fabric. This is especially useful when drawing new design lines. You can also use it to draw a stitching guideline. The marks can be brushed or washed away when you no longer need them for reference.

An **iron, ironing board, and press cloth** are occasionally needed. The iron should have a variety of temperatures and a steam option, necessary for fusing and final pressing of projects. A good pressing can really make a difference in the appearance of the finished project. Protect your project from iron marks and your iron from adhesive residue with a press cloth. The press cloth can be a white fabric remnant; a cloth baby diaper works well, too.

Cutting Tools

Good-quality, sharp **fabric scissors** are a staple. Nothing is more frustrating than trying to cut with a dull pair of scissors. Keep your fabric scissors separate from your household scissors and don't use them to cut paper.

Embroidery scissors—3" or 4" (7.6 or 10.2 cm) with two sharp points—are a dream to use when you are taking apart a seam or trimming little thread ends.

A **seam ripper,** which has a single claw-shaped point, is especially useful for starting to take seams apart at the beginning of a seam or at a seam joining.

A **rotary cutter** is a great tool for cutting straight lines. It has a sharp circular blade and resembles a pizza cutter. It is very sharp, so remember to secure the blade guard when you aren't using it. A **self-healing mat** protects your work surface and a clear plastic ruler helps you cut straight.

Sometimes an old or felted sweater has a dull, pilled surface. Spiff it up by removing dangling fibers with a **sweater shaver.** Keep the shaver on hand for the sweaters in your wardrobe, too.

Adhesives and Stabilizers

Stabilizer is a fabric designed to support fashion fabric or, in these projects, sweater knit fabric under embroidery, appliqué, or any decorative embellishment. It's also great for supporting buttonholes in felted fabric. You can use temporary **water-soluble stabilizer** when you want to stabilize the fabric only during stitching.

Fusible and nonfusible interfacing is a fabric that strengthens and stabilizes a fashion fabric, much like stabilizer. It remains part of the project after it is constructed.

Iron-on adhesive comes in a strip or as a sheet, with or without a backing paper. Paper-backed adhesive is applied in two steps. First, the non-paper side is fused to the project. Then, the paper is removed and a second layer of fabric or trim is fused over it. The iron-on adhesive without paper backing is placed between two pieces of fabric (or fabric and trim) and fused in one step.

Seam sealant is a liquid that dries and hardens to secure thread ends or knots for extra security. It's the perfect solution when there is a thread end that is too short to weave into the fabric or tie into a knot.

Fabric glue is great for holding an appliqué or trim in place so that it doesn't slip or move during top-stitching. To avoid overgluing or dripping onto the project, squeeze glue onto a scrap of paper and use a toothpick to spread it.

Basic Tool Kit

Sweater surgery uses a variety of sewing tools, however, all you need are the following basics and you'll be able to make almost everything in this book, and more!

Basic Sewing Tool Kit

- dressmaker's chalk or a fabric-marking pen
- hand-sewing needles
- fabric scissors
- ruler or measuring tape
- seam ripper
- sewing machine
- straight and safety pins

Taking the Sweater Apart

THERE ARE TWO VERY EASY WAYS to take apart a sweater: you can cut it or take out the stitching at the seams. The best method depends on the design of the new project and the fiber content and construction of the old sweater. For more detailed information to help in the decision making process, read on!

Types of Sweater Seams

Most sweaters are either serged or sewn together with a chain stitch. A serged seam must be cut apart, but a chain stitch pulls apart very easily once you find the right way to pull the thread or yarn (see "When to Take Seams Apart").

A **serged seam** consists of three, four, or five threads and can only be stitched with a serger

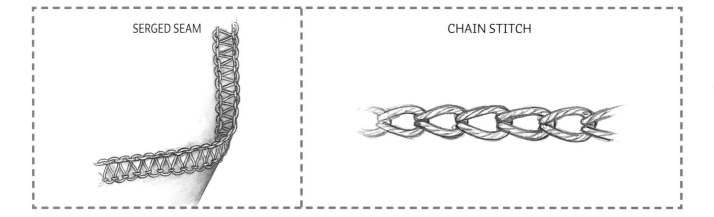

SERGED SEAM

CHAIN STITCH

machine. The serger cuts the sweater fabric as it sews the seam. The edge of the knitted sweater will fall apart and unravel if you remove the serging.

A **chain stitch** is used to construct many commercially machine-knit sweaters. It looks just like a hand-embroidery chain stitch, as well as the stitch that is used to close pet food bags, which is why I affectionately call it the pet food bag stitch! It can be removed all in one step, if you pull the right thread, on the right side, and in the right direction! This is very useful if you want to use the sweater yarn to sew the new project. Practice opening a chain-stitched seam until you find that essential thread.

When to Cut Seams Apart

There are several instances when it is easier to cut the sweater apart rather than open the seams. Cut apart any sweater that has been felted because the fibers are meshed together and won't unravel. Wool felts easily and can be cut apart without raveling.

Cut apart any sweater that has been constructed with serged seams (see "Types of Sweater Seams"). Serging cuts the loops of the knitting along the seam edge as it stitches, so the entire sweater will fall apart if you remove the stitches. You can also cut apart a sweater when the new project doesn't utilize the sewn edges (see "Using Existing Design Elements and Edges") and when the front, back, or sleeve is large enough to provide ample sweater fabric.

If you decide to cut apart the sweater, it's often a good idea to machine stitch around the chosen area before cutting, especially on loose weaves. Cut just outside of your seam; the stitching helps to prevent unraveling, reduces stretching, and acts as a cutting guideline for cutting.

When to Take Seams Apart

Most seams (other than serged seams) come apart simply by pulling a single thread. Start by opening the seam with a seam ripper. Once the beginning of the seam is open, pull one of the threads. If the seam doesn't open easily, pull from the other side of the seam. The entire stitched seam should fall open as you pull the yarn or thread.

Take seams apart when you want to use the edge of the seam as the finished edge of your project and/or when the original seam will be restitched to another part of the sweater to create a new silhouette. You should also take them apart if the area will be visible or exposed.

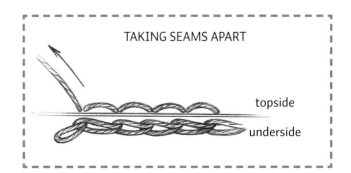

TAKING SEAMS APART

topside

underside

Using Existing Design Elements and Edges

It is fun and easy to incorporate the existing finished edges and design features of the original sweaters in your new project. Take (don't cut) the seams apart, unless the sweater is felted or serged. Ribbed edges at the lower edge of many sweater bodies and sleeve cuffs work nicely in new designs. Collars, knit patterns, pockets, and almost any design element make interesting accents on new projects, such as in the Pom-pom Hat (page 48), the Mittens & Stocking Set (page 40), and the Limelight Purse (page 34). You can also make use of preexisting buttons and closures, as in the Bird-in-Hand Purse (page 28).

Reclaiming Yarn from the Sweater

Sometimes when you refashion a sweater, matching the yarn or thread color exactly is important, but sometimes it doesn't matter. If you want a perfect match, reuse the yarn from the original sweater. This is especially easy when the sweater was sewn with a chain stitch. Take care to open seams so that you have a single or several long lengths of yarn. Wrap the yarn around a small piece of cardboard or a pad of paper to keep it from tangling until you're ready to use it.

If you weren't lucky enough to get several long lengths of thread or yarn when you took the sweater apart at the seams, try unraveling yarn from an unused knitted section, or simply use the closest matching yarn you can find.

Sewing the New Design

YOU CAN SEW THE NEW DESIGN by hand or machine. Either way is fine for most of the projects, but don't shy away from hand sewing just because you think it's tedious or that you're not good at it. All it takes is a little practice and patience.

Hand-Sewing Basics

Most hand stitching, especially when you use matching thread or yarn, blends into the knit fabric and becomes invisible. Hand stitching can be relaxing and meditative, and it's portable! If the stitches are meant to be visible, practice them on a scrap of sweater fabric. Your stitches can be uniform or random and fun. Either way, give it a try, you can always rip out and start again. It's never a one-shot deal!

Stitch with a **single length of thread** when you are working with embroidery floss or when you want a delicate look. Do not knot the thread end because it will pull right through the sweater. Instead, make the first stitch from the wrong side up

through the fabric to the right side and tie a knot with the tail and the working thread, to prevent the knot from slipping through the sweater fabric. To continue the seam, see the stitches on pages 22-25.

HAND STITCHING

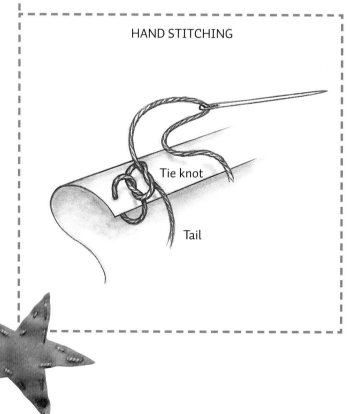

Tie knot

Tail

Stitch with a **double length of thread** when the seam needs to be strong and invisible from the right side of the project. Knot the thread ends together. Insert the needle from the wrong side up to the right side and pull the thread so the knot almost reaches the back of the fabric surface. Insert the needle back through the loop, before the knot, and pull the thread snug. This will prevent the thread from pulling through the sweater. To continue the seam, see stitches on pages 22-25.

Hide the thread ends at the end of hand-stitched seams by running the thread through the thickness of the knit fabric after tying a knot. This leaves the thread tail buried in the stitching and helps to prevent the knot from coming untied.

INSERT THE NEEDLE THROUGH THE LOOP

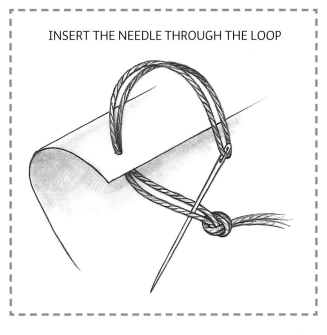

Machine-Sewing Basics

Most sweaters **stretch** unless they have been felted. They tend to stretch more in the width than the length. If you want to maintain the stretch in the new project, join the new pieces with a zigzag or stretch stitch. To prevent the sweater fabric from stretching out of shape, use a stabilizer (see page 15). The stabilizer can be fused or basted to the wrong side of the fabric to prevent it from stretching.

Stitch length is also important. Shorter stitches should be used with fine, lightweight knits and longer stitches on thicker knits. If the ends of a sweater that has been taken apart will show in the new project, sew with short stitches (six to eight stitches per inch) along the newly opened edge.

Basting stitches are long stitches and are used to temporarily hold two pieces together, to gather a larger piece to a smaller piece, and/or to create decorative trim.

If you need **strong, secure seams** to support weight as in a purse, sew two rows of parallel stitches. The second row should be stitched outside the first row, in the seam allowance. Two rows of stitching will also minimize unraveling.

Construction and Decorative

A **basic appliqué stitch** is used to visibly hand sew appliqués in place. Keep stitches equally spaced and consistent in length.

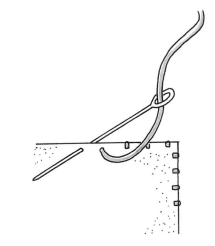

TO HAND STITCH: Bring the needle from the back of the background fabric through the appliqué, $\frac{1}{16}$ to $\frac{1}{8}$ inch (1.6 to 3.2 mm) away from the edge. Reinsert the needle into the background fabric just opposite the thread tail and then back onto the appliqué. Continue working stitches one at a time.

Stitches

Most of these stitches can be done by hand or by machine. Check your sewing machine's owner's manual to learn what stitches are available for your particular model.

The **backstitch** forms a strong, tight, flexible seam. A few backstitches at the beginning and end of a seam will provide extra strength and secure the stitches.

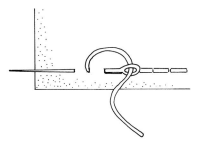

TO HAND STITCH: Take a ⅛ "(3 mm) stitch. Insert the needle behind the thread and take another ¼" stitch. Continue to form a seam.

TO MACHINE STITCH: Take two stitches and then set the machine for reverse and stitch directly over them. Then continue the seam, stitching over the stitches a third time.

Basting stitches work like pins to minimize stretching and temporarily hold pieces together. To baste, handsew a running stitch to hold fabric layers together. You can remove the basting stitches once you have finished sewing the project. You can also use long running stitches to gather a piece of fabric.

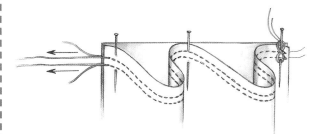

TO HAND OR MACHINE GATHER: Stitch two parallel rows of straight, long stitches, leaving long thread tails. Secure one end of the tails and pull the other ends to gather the fabric. Use a running stitch to baste by hand or a long machine straight stitch to baste by machine.

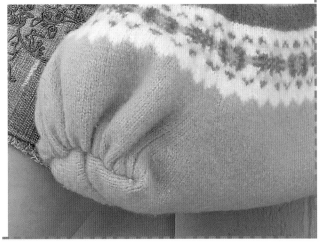

The **blanket stitch** is a nice way to finish an edge or to attach an image, motif, or appliqué onto a background fabric. You can also use it to seam together two sides of a project.

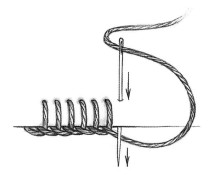

TO HAND STITCH: Working from left to right, insert the needle from the back to the front, the desired distance from the cut fabric edge. Hold the thread so it's behind the point of the needle. Pull the needle through the fabric loop to form a knot along the fabric edge. Space the stitches evenly apart and vary their length for decorative stitching.

The **running stitch** is a row of straight stitches that shows on the top and bottom of the fabric. Use long running stitches to baste the designated area of a sweater, to minimize stretching, or for gathering. Small running stitches can secure a seam and/or be decorative.

TO HAND STITCH: Bring the needle to the right side at the desired location. Insert it in and out of the fabric at even intervals to form several small stitches. Keep the stitch length and the spaces between them the same length.

The **satin stitch** is great for edging an appliqué or creating a wide row of decorative stitching. The machine satin stitch is a series of zigzag stiches that forms a heavy line.

TO HAND STITCH: Bring the needle to the right side and reinsert it across the area to be filled. Slide the needle under the fabric and bring it back to the right side next to the previous stitch. Continue until the area is filled.

The **overcast stitch** wraps around a cut edge to finish and strenghten it, and to minimize raveling.

The **slip stitch** is an almost invisible hand stitch used to join two folded edges.

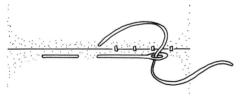

TO HAND STITCH: Insert the needle inside the fabric fold and bring it out through the folded edge. Insert the needle into the fold of the opposite edge and bring it out through the fold, about ¼" (6 mm) away. Repeat, alternating from edge to edge with each stitch.

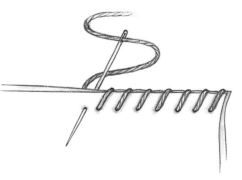

TO HAND STITCH: With the right or wrong sides together, form stitches over the edges of the fabric, ¹⁄₁₆" (1.6 mm) ¼" (6 mm) apart and as deep as necessary to create a firm seam. Work the beginning stitches over the tread tail.

Scarf of Many Colors by
Mindy Relyea, page 52.

THE PROJECTS

Grab your scissors and get cutting!

Now that the basics have been covered, the next step is to give it a try. This section includes a wide variety of projects with step-by-step instructions including cutting diagrams and patterns to guide you seamlessly through the process, or at least with seams straight or curvey as desired. From cute cropped sweaters to little creatures that are sure to put a smile on your face, the following pages will take you through your adventure in deconstructing and reconstructing your own sweater masterpieces.

Note: All projects by the author unless otherwise noted.

Materials

- embroidered cardigan sweater
- matching sewing thread
- trapezoidal-shaped purse handles (Dritz #9898)
- three buttons from JHB #943

Tools

- basic tool kit (page 15)
- three pattern pieces on pages 144-145

Before

A Bird in the Hand Purse

Collecting embroidery can be such fun, but what to do with it? Why not transform the great details found on an outdated sweater into something that provides enjoyment on a daily basis—like this cute purse. There's certainly no point in keeping things tucked away and out of site when you could be giving them new life and new purpose!

Getting Started Enlarge the pattern pieces 200 percent on a photocopy machine. Cut one back piece, one front right, and one front left piece from the sweater to best show the embroidery and to incorporate the button band into the design. Note that the back pattern piece can be folded in half along the center line and pinned along a folded piece of sweater. Once the pieces are cut, transfer the pattern markings to the fabric with chalk, a fabric-marking pen, or with pins.

Step 1 Lap the front left piece over the front right piece with right sides facing up as the pattern indicates. Topstitch along the inner edge of the button band. Backstitch at both ends of the seam.

Step 2 Pin the joined front pieces to the back piece with right sides together. Mark each side with a pin to show where to begin and end stitching, using the pattern as a guide. Machine-stitch from one marking, down the side, across the bottom, and up to the remaining marking. Backstitch at the beginning and end of the seam. Sew a second row of stitches close to the first in the seam allowance for stability and to prevent fraying.

Step 3 Fold and pin the remaining side edge seam allowances to the wrong side handstitch them in place. Fold the top edges to the wrong side at the marking. Place the lower edge of each purse handle under the top folded edge, one on each side. Slip stitch along the fabric edge to encase the handles.

tip

If it's challenging to position the front pattern piece because you can't see the sweater embroidery through it, trace the pattern onto wax paper or tracing paper for greater visibility.

tip

You might want to replace the original buttons with bolder buttons that match the purse handle. Simply resew them directly over the buttonholes.

Materials

· long-sleeved,
  felted pullover sweater
· matching sewing thread
· eight 1" (2.5 cm)-diameter
  brushed silver curtain
  grommets (Dritz #44373)

Tools

· basic tool kit (page 15)

Before

Gathering-Up-the-Goodies Bag

The casual look of a drawstring bag makes it the perfect accessory when you're on the go. Why not combine a felted sweater and unusual hardware, such as curtain grommets, to make a sporty bag.

Getting Started Examine the sweater to determine the best way to use the knit pattern or design. You will need to cut two same-size rectangles. This bag was made from 12 × 14" (30.5 × 35.6 cm) rectangles cut from the front and back of the sweater.

Step 1 With the right sides together, sew down the sides and across the bottom close to the cut sweater edges.

Step 2 To make metered corners on the bottom of the bag, keep the right sides together. At one corner, bring the bottom seam to the side seam and sew across the triangle about 3 to 4" from the corner point. Repeat

for the other corner. Hand stitch the points to the bottom seam of the bag so it is neat inside. Turn the bag right side out.

Step 3 Measure across the top edge of the bag and mark the location of four evenly spaced grommets on each side. To apply the grommets, follow the application instructions on the grommet packaging.

Step 4 Cut a 1- to 1½" (2.5 to 3.8 cm)-wide "coil" strip out of one of the sleeves, as shown in the photograph. Fold or finger press the cut edges to the inside and hand slip stitch the strip

closed to create the drawstring shoulder strap.

Step 5 Thread the strap in and out of each grommet and then hand slip stitch the ends of the strap together.

Materials

- striped felted sweater
- coordinating solid-colored felted sweater
- matching sewing thread
- purse handles: straight rod with D handle 11 ½" × 4 ½" (29.2 × 11.4 cm) (Blumenthal Craft #900019521)
- pin back

Tools

- basic tool kit (page 15)
- glue gun and glue sticks
- patterns (pages 144-145)

Before

Color-Me-Happy Striped Purse

Sassy stripes, whether horizontal or vertical, make a fun purse! This cute purse features vertical stripes with solid color end panels.

Getting Started Enlarge the side panel pattern 200 percent; use it to cut two fabric pieces from the solid felted sweater. Cut two rectangles from the striped fabric as follows: 20 ½" × 13 ½" (52.1 × 34.3 cm) or the length of your purse handle bars plus 2" (5.1 cm).

If the sweater is not large enough to cut the bag piece, cut two pieces (one from the sweater front and one from the sweater back) and sew them together. Remember to add ½" (1.3 cm) to each piece for a seam allowance. The seam should be on the bottom of the bag.

Step 1 Pin the end pieces to the striped bag piece with the right sides together. Because the end pieces are shaped, start pinning at the bottom center and work

toward the ends. Use extra pins around the curves. Machine stitch the seams, taking care not to stretch the fabric. Backstitch at the beginning and end of the seams.

Step 2 Lay the purse handle bars along the top edge of the purse. On both sides of the opening, mark with pins where each handle end meets its handle bar. Cut a slit 1- to 1 ½" (2.5 to 3.8 cm) from the edge inward at the pin marks. Wrap the top edge around the purse handle bar, extending the handles upward through the slits. Slip stitch the slits closed and the top edge to the inside of the bag, encasing the handle bar in the seam. Continue stitching the top edge to the inside, across both side panels.

Step 3 To shape the bag, make a pleat in the center of each end panel by forming a ½" tuck at the center and stitching it closed for about ½" from the top edge.

Step 4 To make the embellishment, cut a strip 1 ½" (3.8 cm) wide by 6 to 7" (15.2 to 17.8 cm) long from the neckline of one of the sweaters. Sew gathering stitches (page 23) along one long edge; pull the threads to form the circle. Stitch the two short ends together to complete the circle. Glue a pin back on the back side of the circle and glue a reclaimed flower button from another sweater onto the front. Pin the embellishment onto the purse.

Materials

- long-sleeved felted sweater with patch pockets
- matching sewing thread
- coordinating pom-poms
- scraps of coordinating felt
- flower-shaped flat button
- pin back

Tools

- basic tool kit (page 15)
- patterns for embellishment (page 145)
- glue gun and glue sticks

Before

Limelight Purse

Purse sides and handle

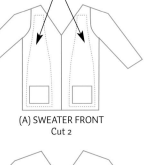

(A) SWEATER FRONT
Cut 2

(B) SWEATER BACK
Cut 1

(C) SWEATER SLEEVE
Cut sleeve open

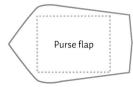

(D) SWEATER SLEEVE
Cut 1

Working with the existing features on a sweater can help you create fabulous recycled projects. Here, a cardigan with pockets becomes a fun and functional purse. Pop on some pom-poms for a bold, funky look. Snip a few scraps into a flower pin for you or for your purse.

Getting Started

The size of the purse is determined by the size of the sweater. Cut the side/handle pieces of the bag from the front of the sweater so that the pockets are along the bottom edge (see diagram A). Cut the body of the bag from the back of the sweater (see diagram B). Open the underarm seam of one sleeve (see diagram C). Cut the flap the same width as the body piece and three-quarters as long (see diagram D).

Step 1 Fold the purse body piece in half from top to bottom to find the center and mark both sides with a pin. Fold the side pieces in half from side to side and mark the center with pins. Pin the body to the sides with the right sides together so that the center pin markings line up and the pockets are visible. Machine stitch the pieces together, pivoting at the corners of the sides and leaving 1"(2.5 cm) unstitched at the beginning and end of the seam to fold to the inside.

Step 2 Fold the top 1" (2.5 cm) of fabric at the beginning and end of the seam to the inside and stitch it in place.

Step 3 Fold the sides of the flap and one end of the flap to the inside 1" (2.5 cm) and hand or machine stitch. Lap the unstitched end to the inside of one side of the purse body and stitch it into place.

Step 4 Fold under the sides of the strap to the desired width and hand stitch them into place. Hand stitch the top ends together.

Step 5 Glue pom-poms onto the edge of the flap, along the top seam of the strap, and in the center of each pocket.

Step 6 Cut two flower shapes from scraps of felt using the patterns on page 147, and glue them together with a pom-pom and button in the center (see photo). Glue a pin on the back and pin the flower to the purse.

Materials

- solid pink felted sweater
- striped pink felted sweater
- matching sewing thread
- silver 2 ⅛" (5.5 cm) rings (Dritz Glamour Rings #121-65)
- silver 1 ⅝" (4.1 cm) buckle (Dritz Buckle #152-65)
- 9" (22.9 cm) pink zipper
- Velcro square or dot

Tools

- basic tool kit (page 15)
- zipper presser foot
- patterns (page 147)

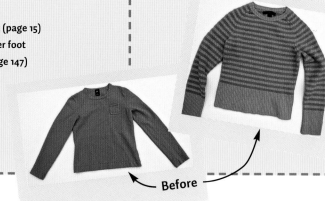

Before

Pink Pizzazz Purse

Tiny purses with details are as much fun to make as they are to carry. This ultra-mod bag is made from solid and striped pink sweaters. It features a tiny pocket that was on the sweater, and a striped strap that is linked to the purse with large fashion rings. The purse has a zipper closure and a buckle strap, added for a decorative, final touch.

tip

No need to attach the soft fuzzy side of the Velcro; the sweater fabric works just as well.

Getting Started

Enlarge the pattern pieces 200 percent and cut them out. Pin the pattern pieces to the felted sweaters as follows.

Pink Sweater: Cut two front/back panel pieces. If the sweater has a cute pocket, cut one panel piece to include it; otherwise, cut a 2" (5.1 cm) square to make a pocket.

Striped Sweater: Cut one bottom piece and one handle piece so that the end of the patterns are placed on a fold of the fabric with the stripes running horizontally. If there isn't a large enough sweater area to cut the bottom in one piece, add ½" (1.3 cm) to the end of the pattern at the fold line, cut second piece, and sew them together. Cut one buckle strap piece, again with the stripes running horizontally.

Step 1 Pin the top edges of the side panel pieces to each side of the zipper (on the zipper

tape) so that the edges meet. Install a zipper presser foot and topstitch the panels to the zipper. If there isn't a pocket on the sweater fabric, topstitch a small pocket on one panel.

Step 2 Open the zipper. Pin the purse bottom to each side of the front/back panels with the right sides together. The narrow ends of the bottom will extend beyond the top edge of the panels. Sew with a ½" (1.3 cm) seam allowance. Take care not to stretch the fabric.

Step 3 Turn the purse right side out. Fold the ends of the

bottom to the inside of the purse and insert a silver ring in each fold. Hand stitch the ends in place.

Step 4 Fold the ends of the purse strap over each ring as shown in the photograph, and hand stitch them closed.

Step 5 Hand stitch the straight end of the buckle band onto the center of the back of the purse. Poke the buckle through the strap near the shaped end. Hand sew or glue the loop side of the Velcro to the back of the buckle strap.

tip

Start sewing the seam at the center of each piece, sewing toward the narrow ends. This will help prevent distorting the fabric pieces.

Cheerleader Purse

This flirty purse is sure to get you noticed. The felted wool is sturdy enough to carry all your necessities and stretchy enough to accommodate a few extras. For a more subdued look, try pairing two sweaters that are closer in tone.

Materials

- turquoise felted sweater with straight, smooth edges and a 3" (7.6 cm) ribbed cuff
- yellow felted sweater
- matching sewing thread
- narrow rickrack
- 1" (2.5 cm)-diameter button

Tools

- basic tool kit (page 15)
- iron and ironing board

Getting Started

Cut the following pieces of felted sweater fabric:

- two 10" × 8½" (25.4 × 21.6 cm) pieces of turquoise fabric
- one 4" × 16" (10.2 × 40.6 cm) piece of turquoise fabric
- one 9" × 5½" (22.9 × 14 cm) piece of yellow fabric
- one 1½" × 16" (3.8 × 40.6 cm) piece of yellow fabric

Step 1 Cut the larger yellow panel into triangular sections, as shown in the illustration. [5½" (14 cm), 9" (22.9 cm)]

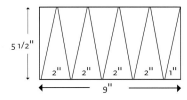

Step 2 With a ruler and fabric-marking pen, draw cutting lines extending from the nonribbed edge of both of the larger turquoise pieces. The lines should be 2" (5.1 cm) apart and 5 1/2" (14 cm) long, as shown in the illustration. Cut along the markings.

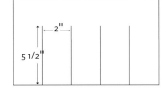

Step 3 Spread the turquoise panel open at the cut lines and, with the wrong sides together, pin a yellow triangle into each opening. Machine stitch all the yellow inserts with a ⅛"(3 mm) seam allowance, backstitching at the beginning and end of the seams. Press with a steam iron set to the wool temperature setting.

Step 4 Pin together the newly formed panels, with the right sides together along the sides and bottom. Carefully align and pin the bottom edge. Machine stitch with a ¼" (6 mm) seam allowance. Turn the purse right side out.

Step 5 Assemble the strap by pinning the long edge of the remaining yellow piece to the long edge of the remaining turquoise piece, with the wrong sides together. Stitch with a ¼" (6 mm) seam allowance. Repeat with the other two long edges, to form a tube. Resist the urge to turn the tube wrong side out, since the seams are a decorative element. Press the tube so that the yellow section runs down the center of the strap. Measure and pin every 4" (10.2 cm). Fold the seam allowances toward each other so they meet at every 4" pin marking and pin them together. Machine or hand stitch back and forth several times across each pinned location. This will create a wavy, 3-D effect for the handle.

Step 6 Pin the handle to the inside of the purse at the side seams, 1" (2.5 cm) from the top edge. Machine stitch each end in place with a double row of stitching, for stability.

Step 7 Hand sew the button to the front of the purse, 1½" (3.8 cm) from the top edge. Back the button with a small scrap of felted wool on the inside, for reinforcement.

Step 8 Fashion a button loop from an 8" (20.3 cm) piece of rickrack. Fold the rickrack in half to form a point. Pin the point in place and hand stitch back and forth to secure it. Stitch the two pieces of rickrack ¾" (1.9 cm) and 2" (5.1 cm) from the point, to form the buttonhole. Stitch the opposite end of the rickrack to the back side of the purse, opposite the button, 1" (2.5 cm) from the top edge.

Materials

· felted sweater with ribbed edge
· matching sewing thread

Tools

· basic tool kit (page 15)
· patterns (page 148)

Before

Merry Mittens & Stocking Set

Holiday gifts are extra special when you make them yourself. Dress your friends with a warm and toasty pair of mittens made from a Fair Isle sweater. And, deck their halls with a colorful stocking. Surprise them by making it from one of their own, old, well-loved sweaters. They'll be amazed by how you were able to transform a sweater into a charming holiday accessory and they'll think of you whether they're at home or on the go!

Getting Started on Mittens

Trace your hand and add ½" (1.3 cm) all the way around, or enlarge the pattern on page 148 to fit your hand. Place the wrist edge of the pattern on the bottom edge of the sleeve (if it fits), sweater front, or sweater back. A rib-edged sweater will have a bit more give than one without a ribbed edge. Pin the pattern to two sweater layers with the wrong sides together. Any design in the sweater should be the same on both layers. Cut out the first mitten pieces. Repeat for the second mitten.

Mitten Instructions

Step 1 Pin the layers with the right sides together. Machine stitch around, close to the cut edge. Backstitch at the beginning and end of the seam. Pivot at the interior thumb point. After you are finished stitching the seam, clip up to the stitching at the pivot point, through the seam allowance. Turn the mittens right side out. If the ribbed section is wide enough, fold it back to form a cuff.

Getting Started on Matching Holiday Stocking

Enlarge the stocking pattern 400 percent on a photocopy machine. Place the top edge of the stocking pattern on the ribbed area of the sweater. Cut a double layer with the wrong sides together, or cut a single layer and flop the pattern piece before cutting the second layer, to get a mirror image.

Matching Holiday Stocking Instructions

Step 1 Pin the stocking pieces with the right sides together. Mark the foldline for the cuff.

Machine stitch around the edge of the stocking, starting and stopping at the marked foldline. Backstitch at the beginning and end of the seam.

Step 2 Turn the stocking right side out and stitch the cuff side seams together on each side of the stocking, as the pattern indicates. Fold the cuff over.

Step 3 Cut from the sweater a 1 ½ × 4 ½" (3.8 × 11.4 cm) strip of felted wool. Sew it lengthwise to form a tube. Hand sew the tube inside the heel side of the stocking to make a hanging loop.

Before

Zap & Shine Felted Pink Mittens

These graphic pink mittens were cut from the sleeves of a bright pink wool sweater that was picked up at a local thrift store. The motifs are cut from scraps of a white wool sweater. Both sweaters were only slightly felted so that the mittens are pliable enough to open door handles and pack snowballs!

tip

Stitch a piece of yarn the length of your arms from wrist to wrist inside the wrist of each paired mitten. Run the yarn through the arms of your coat and you'll never lose your fabulous new mittens!

Getting Started Trace your hand and add ½" (1.3 cm) all the way around, or enlarge the pattern on page 149 on a photocopy machine to fit your hand. Place the wrist edge of the pattern on the bottom edge of the sleeve (if it fits, otherwise pin it on the front or back of the sweater along the ribbed edge). A rib-edged sweater will have a bit more give than one without a ribbed edge. Pin the pattern to the two sweater layers, with the wrong sides together. Cut out two sets of mittens. Cut out one star and one lightning bolt appliqué (page 148) from the white sweater. Or, you can use any appliqué shapes; just draw them on paper first to make sure they fit on the mitten.

Step 1 Place both sets of cut mittens on the table so that thumbs are pointing toward each other, to ensure that you appliqué on the right side and back (not palms) of each mitten. Glue a shape onto each top mitten piece. After the glue has dried, the appliqués are ready to embellish with little sparkly stitches.

Step 2 Cut a length of embroidery floss about 18"

(45.7 cm) long. Work with a single length of thread and hand stitch around the appliqués with the basic appliqué stitch (page 22) or another stitch of your choice.

Step 3 Once the appliqués are attached, flip the mitten pieces so the right sides are together. Pin around the edges. Machine stitch close to the cut edge. Backstitch at the beginning and end of the seam. Pivot at the inside thumb point. After stitching, clip a small slit at the inside thumb point, through the seam allowance up to the stitching. Turn the mittens right side out.

tip

If fibers from the underside of the fabric are poking through to the top-side, reverse the stitches. Bring your needle up through the single outside layer and down through the appliqué.

Materials for White Booties

- white felted sweater
- 6 star-shaped buttons
- matching sewing thread

Tools

- basic tool kit (page 15)
- pattern (page 149)

Before

Baby's Got the '80s Goin' on Booties

Baby booties are so cute, who can resist them? Those of us that remember the ultra-cool white boots from the '80s will get a kick out of these mini retro booties. Star buttons and fringe will have baby smilin'. Little buckaroos will be tappin' toes with the mini cowboy version. Hand-sewn appliqués give them Western style.

Getting Started on White Booties Determine how much to enlarge the upper boot and two sole patterns by placing the baby's correct size shoe on the pattern over the shoe drawing. Keep enlarging the patterns on a photocopy machine until the shoe drawing and actual shoe are the same size. Cut around the outside lines of the pattern pieces. Lay the sweater on the table with the arms extended straight out. Position the upper bootie pattern along the armhole seam and the side seam (see diagram A). Repeat for the second bootie at the other armhole/side seam. Trace around the pattern with a fabric-marking pen or pin the patterns in place. Cut out the pieces. Cut two sets of soles from the remaining area of the sweater.

Step 1 Use the pattern as reference and with the right sides together, sew the front/top of the bootie to form the toe. Trim off any extra seam allowance.

Step 2 With the right sides together, beginning at the side, sew the sole to the upper bootie. Continue stitching so that the (continued on page 46)

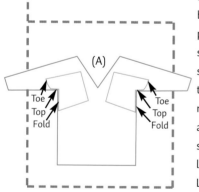

(A)

Toe
Top
Fold

Toe
Top
Fold

upper bootie overlaps itself. Repeat for the other bootie/sole so that the fabric overlaps in the opposite direction. Sew through all three fabric layers at the overlapped area.

Step 3 Turn the booties right side out. Sew the three buttons 1" (2.5 cm) from the edge along the inside flap. Snip a corresponding vertical slit for each buttonhole on the outside flap.

Step 4 Snip the outside overlapping flap horizontally ¼ to ½" (6 mm to 2.5 cm) up to make the fringe. Snip each fringe end into a point.

Materials for Red Booties

· red felted sweater
· cream felted sweater scraps
· matching sewing thread
· dark red embroidery floss
· six ½" (1.3 cm)-diameter
  cream buttons
· four ⅛" (3 mm)-diameter
  cream buttons

Tools for Red Booties

· basic tool kit (page 15)
· patterns (page 149)

Before

Toe Tappin' Booties

Getting Started on Red Booties

Enlarge the bootie and appliqué patterns the same percentage and follow the same directions as for the white booties, but cut the top edge in a curve, as the pattern indicates. Cut two sets of boot appliqués. Cut four ½ × 2" (1.3 × 5.1 cm) boot straps.

Step 1 Follow the same instructions as for the white booties, steps 1–4.

Step 2 Fold each strap in half and stitch to encase top edge of bootie at each side with a tiny button. Pin the appliqués to the outside of the booties. Stitch them in place with a tiny running stitch and a single strand of contrasting embroidery floss.

Materials

- unfelted sweater with optional contrast rib trim
- matching sewing thread
- scraps of color coordinating felt
- 2 large pom-poms and coordinating yarn
- 1 small pom-pom pin back

Tools

- basic tool kit (page 15)
- glue gun and glue sticks
- paper pattern for flower accent (page 150)

Before

Pom-pom Hat

Warm and stylish at the same time! This hat will put a smile on your face, with dangling pom-poms that swing around with your every movement. Make a coordinating flower accent with pieces of felt that match the colors of the hat.

Getting Started

To determine the size of the hat, measure your head. Add 1" (2.5 cm) to this measurement for the seam allowances, to determine the total width of the piece you'll need to cut. You can also wrap the lower edge of the sweater around your head to double-check the measurement. Sweaters stretch differently, which affects how snugly the hat will fit.

Mark the desired width along the lower edge of the sweater (see diagram A). Measure and mark 15" (38.1 cm) up from the lower edge several times for the height of the hat. Cut the sweater along the markings (see diagram A).

Step 1 Fold the rectangle in half widthwise with the right sides together. Hand or machine stitch the seam.

Step 2 Draw a curve from the top of one side to the opposite side with chalk (see diagram B), using a plate or shaped ruler as a guide. Pin the top layers with the wrong sides together along the curve. Machine stitch; backstitch at the beginning and end of the seam. Trim away the excess fabric and turn the hat right side out.

Step 3 Cut two pieces of yarn, each about 4" (10.2 cm) long. Knot one end and use a hand-sewing needle to run the opposite end of yarn from the inside, through the point of the hat. Repeat with remaining piece of yarn. Glue a large pom-pom onto each yarn end.

Step 4 Cut three different color pieces of felt, using the pattern on page 150. Glue them together with the largest piece on the bottom and the little pom-pom on top. Glue the bottom layer to the pin back. Fold up the cuff of the hat and hold it in place with the pin.

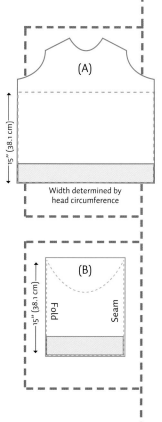

(A)

15" (38.1 cm)

Width determined by head circumference

(B)

15" (38.1 cm)

Fold

Seam

Materials

- 8 felted sweaters cut into 6" × 7 ½" (15.2 × 19.1 cm) pieces
- 3 remnants for appliqués, approximately 3 ½" (8.9 cm) square
- ¾" (1.9 cm)-diameter button
- coordinating embroidery floss

Tools

- scissors
- embroidery needle

Scarf of Many Colors

Rectangles of vibrantly patterned and solid-colored sweaters are stitched together make playful scarves that are sure to brighten even the coldest and dreariest day. And, they make good use of felted remnants and leftover bits from other projects! A tiny pocket, decorative hand stitching, crocheted edging, and a keyhole opening are the accents that make this scarf so unique.

tip

The pocket is perfect for a special hidden surprise.

Step 1 Lay out the eight sweater pieces to determine the most pleasing pattern. If any of the sweater pieces are ribbed, use them for the ends.

Step 2 Hand sew the scarf pieces together with any of the decorative stitches shown on pages 22–25.

Step 3 Cut (freehand) a small star from one of the remnants. Sew it in the center of one of the end pieces with a visible running stitch (page 24) and contrast embroidery floss.

Step 4 Cut a pocket from another remnant and hand sew it with visible running stitches to the other end piece. Sew the button in the center, near the top edge of the pocket. Cut a triangular piece for the pocket flap from the remaining remnant. Lay it over the pocket and adjust the size as needed. Cut a vertical slit in the pocket to fit the button. Hand sew the flap in place.

DESIGNED BY MINDY RELYEA

Materials

- 20 felted 4" (10.2 cm) sweater squares
- ¼ yard (22.9 cm) coordinating cotton fabric
- matching sewing thread
- 1 skein variegated crewel or embroidery thread

Tools

- basic tool kit (page 15)
- embroidery needle
- I/9 crochet hook (optional)

tip

The looser the buttonhole stitch, the easier it is to lay the squares flat.

Keyhole Scarf

The keyhole in this patchwork scarf lets you wear it close to snuggle your neck and keep away the winter chill. Use a variegated crewel or embroidery thread to add flair to the stitching.

Step 1 Lay out the felted squares, two to a row, to achieve a color pattern that you like. With the wrong sides together, blanket stitch (page 24) the squares together with the decorative thread.

Step 2 Cut the lining fabric the same size as the joined squares. Machine sew the lining and patchwork fabric with the wrong sides together and a ¼" (6 mm) seam allowance. Leave an opening 8" (20.3 cm) long.

Step 3 Turn the scarf right side out and slip stitch (page 24) the scarf closed. Blanket stitch the perimeter of the scarf with the decorative thread.

Step 4 To make the keyhole, machine or hand stitch a 4" (10.2 cm) horizontal buttonhole across the center of the second row of patches. Carefully cut the buttonhole open. If you want, finish the scarf with several rows of crochet edging.

Materials

- large white sweater with vertical bobble and textured pattern
- matching sewing thread

Tools

- basic tool kit (page 15)
- yarn needle (page 14)

Before

Snow White Scarf

Bobbles and cables are some of the best knitting textures. Take advantage of those complicated stitches when they're already knit in a big, old oversized sweater to get a fun and funky new accessory. Fringing is just as easy as turning and hemming sweater edges, so why not complement the surface texture with kinetic edges.

tip

Vary the width of the fringed edges by cutting closer or farther away from the stitching lines.

Getting Started

Examine the sweater to determine which row of knit stitches you want to make into a scarf. Mark a vertical line (stitching lines) on each side of the chosen bobble pattern with pins or dressmaker's chalk. Mark additional vertical lines out from the first lines (cutting lines) to allow fabric for fringing. Include the sweater cuff or ribbed hem in at least two strips. Mark enough strips (with the same bobble pattern) to make the scarf the desired length.

Step 1 Sew a straight line of short, machine stitches along the inside, marked lines. The unraveling, or fringing, will stop at these stitched lines.

Step 2 After sewing all of the marked stitches, cut the strips along the cutting lines.

Step 3 Sew a stabilizing row of stitches across the narrow ends. This leaves a small bit of yarn at each end to duplicate the fringed feeling of the sides.

Step 4 Lay out the strips so that the two ends of the scarf are the ribbed cuff or hem. Using either reclaimed yarn and a yarn needle or sewing thread and a sewing needle, stitch the ends of the strips together with the wrong sides together, so the seam becomes part of the design. Gather (page 23) the seams to create shape and add a design feature. Fluff the horizontal seams and the raw edges to release the knit stitches. Trim as needed.

Before

Peppermint Patti Swirl Necklace

You don't generally think of mixing sweaters and jewelry in the same project, but why not? These funky little swirls are made with narrow, contrasting color strips of sweaters coiled together. A length of wire (in this case, 26 gauge) is threaded through the swirls amid assorted beads. Colorful suede cording and a big glass bead complete the design.

Getting Started

Cut strips of felted sweaters about ½" (1.3 cm) wide and as long as possible out of the sweater pieces. For swirls about 1" (2.5 cm) in diameter, you will need strips 4 to 5" (10.2 to 12.7 cm) long. For larger swirls that are about 2" (5.1 cm) in diameter, the strips need to be 11 to 13" (27.9 to 35.6 cm) long.

Step 1 To form the swirl, wrap the end of one strip over the edge of the second strip and coil it around. Continue coiling the strips until the swirl is the desired size. Cut the outside strip ⅜" (1 cm) longer than the underside strip. Use a straight pin to hold the swirl closed. Repeat to make as many swirls as you want.

Step 2 Refer to the photograph for inspiration or follow the design of your choice. Begin with a long piece of wire. Cut one end at a sharp angle so it will poke through the sweater swirl. Form a loop at the opposite end. Poke the sharp end of the wire through the swirl from side to side and remove the straight pin. Alternate putting swirls and beads on the wire. When finished, cut the wire to ½" (1.3 cm) and form a loop.

Step 3 Assemble the necklace, interspersing jump rings, beads, and swirls to suit your taste. Finish by tying a double length of cording to jump rings on opposite ends of the wired swirl/bead design. You can even slide a bead onto the cording for the final touch.

Before

Green-with-Envy Necklace

This necklace randomly mixes wool sweater swirls with different style beads. A supersize swirl becomes a pendant with a large chunky glass bead on top and a delicate dangle below. We used two different-weight sweaters; the light green was slightly heavier than the dark green. The possibilities are endless!

Getting Started

See Getting Started on page 57.

Step 1 Follow step 1 on page 59 to make the sweater swirls.

Step 2 Finish each swirl by inserting a length of wire through the center and using the round-nose pliers to form a loop at each end of the wire.

Step 3 Assemble the necklace, alternating sweater swirls, beads, and chain links. Form a pendant in the center with a bead link, a large swirl, and a bead dangle. Add a chain to each end of the bead and swirl section to form the back of the necklace, with a clasp on one end. Remember, the design is up to you!

Materials

- felted sweater scraps
- 10 to 12 beads with 1" (2.5 cm) diameter
- ¾ yard (68.6 cm) tiger-tail beading wire
- 2 crimp beads
- 1 or 2 soldered jump rings
- 1 or 2 open jump rings
- 5–10" (12.7–25.4 cm) of jewelry chain
- S-style hook to fit through jewelry chain and close necklace
- embroidery floss, yarn, or thread
- template plastic or heavyweight paper
- circular template the desired size of felt circles

Tools

- embroidery needle
- scissors
- needle-nose pliers or crimp tool
- wire cutter
- permanent marker
- necklace design board (optional)

Jujube Necklace

What a wild and wooly way to wear a sweater! Make a super-simple necklace with giant beads and felt circles in all the gorgeous colors that come from felted sweaters. Try to use various shades of one color as well as a variety of darks and lights to create depth and interest. Experiment with different-size beads and circles. Look for vintage beads, wooden beads, or even handmade polymer clay beads. Cut your felt circles from one single felted sweater that has a fabulous color pattern, or from a combination of felted sweater remnants. The instructions that follow are for the necklace shown here. Change the number, size, color of the beads, and felt circles to make the design your own!

Getting Started

Find a circular item, such as a coin, lid, or candle, that is the size you want to make the felt circles. Trace around the object onto template plastic or heavy paper to create your template. Cut it out. If your template is clear, it's easier to place it exactly where you want to cut, especially on a patterned sweater. Cut fifty-five or more felt circles in a variety of colors. It's nice to have extra circles in different colors as you design your necklace. If your fabric is fuzzy, hold the template in place and cut around it as you hold it. Snip continuously to keep the edges smooth. Once the circle is cut, trim away uneven edges. If the sweater felt isn't fuzzy, trace around the template and cut the circle, eliminating the marked line as you cut.

Step 1 Plan the necklace by laying out the beads on the design board or on a solid-colored cloth. Between the beads, position "felt sandwiches" made of five different color circles. Experiment with the bead/felt composition by scattering dark (and light)-colored

tip

Leave the wire attached to the spool so the beads don't fall off accidentally.

the remaining crimp bead onto the wire, then through the last link of the jewelry chain and back through the crimp bead. Tighten the crimp bead against the chain, compressing the felt to make the necklace snug. Close the crimp bead with the pliers or crimp tool. Thread the wire back through the last bead, and trim it close to the bead.

Step 6 Decide how many links you need in the jewelry chain so the necklace is the desired length. Usually 3 to 4" (7.6 to 10.2 cm) of chain are enough. Cut the chain to the desired length with the wire cutter.

Step 7 Assemble one last felt circle sandwich. Thread the embroidery needle with embroidery floss or thread. Sew through the center of the sandwich, leaving a 3" (7.6 cm) tail. Tie a soldered jump ring with the floss or thread on both sides of the sandwich. Sew through the sandwich and jump rings three or four times and then secure the thread with a knot. The knot can be decorative, if desired.

Step 8 Attach the sandwich "charm" to the free end of the chain with an open jump ring. Wear the necklace by placing the S-hook through the chain so the necklace is the desired length.

circles and beads throughout the necklace. The felt will compress slightly over time, so make the necklace a little longer than you want. Finish each end with a bead.

Step 2 Once you are satisfied with the design, unwind the beading wire. Extend the wire the desired length of the necklace, plus about 9" (22.9 cm). Leave the wire attached to the spool so the beads don't fall off accidentally. Put the first bead on the wire.

Step 3 To get the felt circles on the wire, thread the end of the wire through the embroidery needle. Hold the first felt sand-wich (five felt circles) in one hand and push the needle through the center so it comes out the other side. Make sure the felt circles are centered on the wire. Then, thread the second bead onto the wire. Remove the needle to thread the beads if the bead holes are too small to fit the needle; otherwise, keep working with the needle. Repeat until the whole necklace is on the wire. Check the length by holding it around your neck.

Step 4 Cut a single link from the jewelry chain with the wire cutters. Push the beads and felt circles away from the free end of the wire. Thread a crimp bead onto the wire. Thread the wire through the single chain link, and back through the crimp bead. Tighten the crimp bead up against the chain link and close the crimp bead with needle-nose pliers or a crimp tool.

Thread the end of the wire through the first bead to hide it by gently pushing the beads toward the opposite end. Trim the wire close to the bead. Attach the S-hook to the chain, using an open jump ring if necessary.

Step 5 To finish the other end, cut the beading wire off the spool, allowing an extra 6" (15.2 cm) to work with. Thread

Materials

- 4" × 25" (10.2 × 63.5 cm) unfelted wool sweater
- matching sewing thread
- two 15" (38.1 cm) lengths of ⅝" (1.6 cm)-wide double-faced satin ribbon
- acid dyes and mordants

Tools

- basic tool kit (page 15)
- pattern (see page 151)
- usual dye supplies (pot, spoons, etc)
- paintbrush or eyedroppers

Twiggy Headband

DESIGNED BY ANNE KUO LUKITO

These totally modern headbands have flair and sass. The striped one is made from the neck of a turtleneck sweater that was hand painted with rainbow colors and then felted! Coordinating satin ribbon ties add extra style. You can even embroider the headband with a simple blanket stitch or personalized motif to make it uniquely yours.The white headbands (see page 131) are just as easy to make.

Getting Started

Enlarge the pattern 200 percent and cut it out.

Step 1 Presoak the sweater fabric for greater dye absorption. Prepare and mix the dyes in a nonreactive shallow pan. Add ½ teaspoon of citric acid or vinegar to the dye mix to prevent the dye from running. Place the fabric in hot water with the right side facing up with enough water to cover the fabric. Paint stripes on the fabric with squirt bottles, eyedroppers, or a paintbrush. Once the desired colors have been applied and the water is clear, carefully remove the sweater. Additional resources on dyeing and hand painting wool can be found in books and online.

Step 2 Felt the dyed fabric in the washing machine (page 12). Once it has felted, block the fabric flat (page 11) and allow it to dry.

Step 3 Fold the fabric in half with the right sides together. Pin the headband pattern on the fold. Trace and cut the pattern.

Step 4 Turn under 1" (2.5 cm) at one end of both pieces of ribbon. Hand or machine sew the turned under ribbon to the wrong side of the headband at each narrow end. Tie the ribbons to wear the headband!

Materials

· plaid long-sleeved cardigan sweater
· matching sewing thread
· matching yarn
· $\frac{1}{16}$" (1.6 mm)-wide elastic

Tools

· basic tool kit (page 15)
· yarn needle (page 14)

Before

Forever-Plaid Skirt

Although plaid sweaters may be relegated to the golf course, a girl can't go wrong bringing the look to the street with a little plaid miniskirt. This skirt design is easy to make and fun to wear. Simply cut the sleeves off and use one of the sleeves as the center front underlay. The lower body of the sweater becomes the skirt!

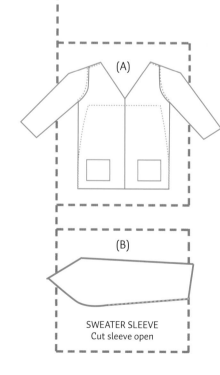

(A)

(B)

SWEATER SLEEVE
Cut sleeve open

Getting Started

Refer to the cutting diagram and use a ruler and fabric-marking pen to draw the design lines of the skirt on the body of the sweater (see diagram A). The lower edge of the sweater and one sleeve will be the hem of the skirt. Use as much of the sweater as you can; you can always shorten the skirt at the waistline later.

If the sweater seems like it will ravel, machine stitch along the marked lines prior to cutting. Cut the sleeves off the sweater, close to the armhole seams, and cut open the shoulder seams. Pin the sweater closed. Snip off any buttons that are in the way. You can always sew them back on when the skirt is finished. Pin the front and back of the sweater together. Cut along the marked design lines through both layers. The sweater will still be partially connected at the lower side seams (see diagram A).

Step 1 Cut one sleeve open along the underarm seam. Save the other sleeve for patchwork or remnant projects (see diagram B).

Step 2 Position the open sleeve so it forms a triangular underlay at the center opening. Align the lower edges. Adjust and pin the side seams to form an A-line skirt shape. Try on the skirt. You will be using elastic at the waist, so adjust the side seams for fit and shorten the skirt by cutting it at the waist to the desired length.

Step 3 When you like the way the skirt fits, topstitch the sleeve panel in place. Sew the side seams with the right sides together. Machine stitch the waist edge with a medium zigzag stitch to prevent raveling.

tip

If the sweater had buttonholes, a few little hand stitches with matching thread will close them up as if they were never there.

Step 4 Create a casing for the waist elastic and a decorative finished edge by whip-stitching the edge with yarn and very close stitches. Cut a piece of elastic equal to your waist measurement. Attach a small safety pin to one end and insert the elastic through the yarn casing on the inside of the skirt. Pin the elastic ends together and try on the skirt. Tighten the elastic as desired.

Step 5 Pull the ends of the elastic out and hand sew them together. Hide the ends back in the casing.

Materials

- solid-color tank-top sweater (unfelted)
- color-coordinating, printed long-sleeved sweater (unfelted)
- sweater or fabric remnant for the belt (felted)
- matching sewing thread
- fusible web
- water-soluble stay tape (optional)
- matching embroidery floss (optional)
- 1" (2.5 cm)-diameter decorative button (La Mode #20947)
- ⅝" (1.6 cm)-diameter snap

Tools

- basic tool kit (page 15)
- iron, ironing board, and press cloth
- shank or wire cutters
- craft glue

Before

Floral Jumper & Super-Skinny Belt

If you like to wear these components as sweaters, you might like them even better when you combine them to make a trendy new and comfy jumper! A basic tank sweater becomes the top, while a bold print sweater is used for the skirt. Make a fabric belt from a third sweater or a remnant, using a glamorous button for a touch of sophistication.

(A)

CUTTING GUIDE FOR
BOTTOM HALF OF JUMPER

(B)

Waist

Side

Side

Front Hem

Getting Started

Decide how long you want to make the jumper and how long you want the bodice to be. It helps to measure a favorite dress or jumper, or to try on the tank-top sweater and pin the other sweater to it. Mark the desired bodice/skirt seam with pins and then measure.

Once you have decided on the length and proportion of the jumper, mark the tank-top sweater at the desired length, adding ½" (1.3 cm) for a seam allowance. Cut along the mark-

ing. Save the bottom half of the sweater for the belt or other projects. To cut the sweater for the bottom of the jumper, refer to diagram A. Cut the front and back of the sweater into large trapezoidal shapes the desired length of the skirt plus ½" (1.3 cm) for a seam allowance. The hem of the sweater will become the hemline of the jumper. Adjust the cutting lines so that the top of both the front and back trapezoid pieces equal half the bottom cut edge of the tank top. Cut both sleeves open at the underarm seams. Cut trian-

gles from each sleeve so they are the same length as the front and back trapezoids and so the bottom cuffs of each sleeve become part of the skirt hem (see diagram B).

Step 1 Pin a sleeve to each side of the front with the right sides together and the original hem and cuff together at the lower edge, as shown in diagram B. Machine stitch, starting at the hem edge, so the bottom edge is smooth and even. Backstitch at the beginning and end of the seam. Repeat by sewing the

tip

If the seams stretch during stitching, baste or fuse wash-away stay tape to the seam.

other side of the sleeves to the back, to form a continuous skirt piece.

Step 2 Use pins to mark the center of the front and back of both the top and the skirt sections. Pin the sweater top to the sweater bottom with their center markings aligned. Ease the fabric so the two sections fit together; pull and stretch them as needed to even out any circumference differences, and pin the seam at regular intervals.

Step 3 Machine sew the top to the bottom with a zigzag stitch. It is important to retain flexibility in this seam. Press all seams gently.

Step 4 Cut a 2" (5.1 cm) wide piece of felted sweater fabric to the measurement of your waist or wherever the belt will be worn, plus 2" (5.1 cm) in length. You might need to cut multiple strips to obtain the correct

length; if so, sew them together at 45-degree angles to reduce bulk.

Press each cut edge ½" (1.3 cm) to the wrong side to create a 1" (2.5 cm)-wide belt. Slide a piece of fusible web inside the belt and fuse the layers together. Whipstitch the cut edges closed.

Step 5 Try on the belt with the dress to find the best length. Trim the belt ends if necessary (and overcast stitch the cut ends) so they overlap about 1" (2.5 cm). Sew a snap onto the ends of the belt. Snip the shank off the back of a decorative button and glue it onto the top end of the belt.

Step 6 Sew thread loops slightly larger than the width of the belt onto the sides of the dress at the seam, using matching embroidery thread or a double strand of sewing thread.

Materials

- raglan-sleeved hoodie sweater with stitched (not serged) seams
- reclaimed yarn or matching thread

Tools

- basic tool kit (page 15)
- yarn needle (page 14)

Before

Green Hoodie

If you don't need or want a big, bulky sweater, but you don't want your arms to get chilly, this little shrug is the perfect in-between garment: warmth for the extremities, without the bulk! This is a great design for a sweater that might have had an unfortunate run-in with food or is starting to come apart at the seams—unintentionally, that is.

tip

To prevent the hood from rolling and the seam from being exposed, hand sew a few backstitches from the back through the sleeve and folded edge of the hood, to keep the hood edge flat. (Work the stitches in the back half of the knit stitches so they don't show on the right side.)

Getting Started

Take the sweater apart at the hood seam and the sleeve seams. You will use only the hood and sleeves. Save the rest of the sweater for a different project.

Step 1

Create a center back seam by using safety pins to pin together the top edge of both sleeves (former neckline seams) with the right sides together. Pin the hood to the joined sleeves, matching the center back of the hood with the new center back sleeve seam. Try on the new garment to see how it fits. Make any fit adjust-ments by stretching or gathering the seams. When you are happy with the fit, take the garment off and repin the new seams so that the sides are symmetrical.

Step 2

Hand stitch the center back sleeve seam first with the right sides together. Then stitch the sleeve section to the hood as it is pinned. Taper and roll the ends of the hood toward the inside of the sleeves, to hide the ends.

Variation: Cool Cabled Hoodie

The white hoodie is just a bit different from the green hoodie. In this case, the sleeves were shorter, so they were stitched to the ends of the hood section. (They don't meet in the back to form a back seam.)

Materials

- turtleneck sweater
- with raglan sleeves
- (not felted)
- measurements taken
- from the sweater

Tools

- seam ripper
- embroidery scissors
- yarn needle

Before

Toasty Turtleneck Shrug

What do you do when you want to keep both your arms and your neck warm? Recycle a turtleneck sweater with raglan sleeves into this sporty shrug. This shrug lets you to show off a funky T-shirt while keeping you warm and comfy.

Getting Started

Take apart the sweater at the neck and the raglan seams. You won't need the sweater front or back pieces (save them for another project). Keep the turtleneck and sleeves.

Step 1 Slip on the turtleneck and sleeves and safety pin them together so that the new shrug fits comfortably. Take off the shrug and adjust the pins so the new seam and sleeves are symmetrical.

Step 2 Lap the sleeves under the neck and hand stitch on the underside along the edge, for a smooth, flat lapped seam. You might find there is extra sleeve fabric at the neck; trim it away. A second row of stitching makes a more secure seam.

tip

Sometimes, the turtleneck section doesn't have a seam because it is knit directly to the body of the sweater. Simply determine the last row of stitches in the body of the sweater and cut them to release the intact neck stitches.

Materials

- 5 wool or wool-blend sweaters, varying in color and pattern
- matching sewing thread
- 2 different trims to be used along the sweater front
- extra large pom-pom or other novelty trim for the neckline
- 5" × 3" (12.7 × 7.6 cm) black or blue felt remnant
- scraps of sweater fabric for appliqués
- embroidery thread in contrasting colors
- 1 ⅝" (1.6 cm)-diameter shank button

Tools

- basic tool kit (page 15)
- patterns (page 156)
- embroidery needle
- serger (optional)
- iron, ironing board, press cloth

DESIGNED BY MINDY RELYEA

Pom-pom Sweater

It's easy to up-cycle thrift-store, wool or wool-blend sweaters by transforming them into fun little children's sweaters. The possibilities are truly endless; it's all up to you and the sweaters you choose. Bold stripes, polka dots, and very bright solids in contrast colors work great together. Cardigans are perfect year-round sweaters and they go with anything from skirts to jeans. The best part: they're truly one of a kind!

Getting Started

Enlarge the sweater front, back, sleeve, and appliqué patterns by the same percentage as needed to fit. It helps to enlarge the front pattern piece and lay it over a cardigan that you own until it is close to the same size. Pin the back, front, and sleeve patterns to different, unfelted sweaters. Cut out one sweater back with the center back along a fold in the sweater fabric. From different fabrics, cut two sweater fronts to be mirror images of each other. Cut two sleeves, placing the wrist end of the pattern on the sleeve cuff and the upper edge of the pattern on a folded edge.

Seam all the sweater pieces with the right sides together, taking care not to stretch the pieces. A machine stretch stitch or a zigzag stitch minimizes stretching. Backstitch at the beginning and end of the seams and steam press as you go. If you own a serger, use it to sew the seams and finish the raw edges. You can also use a sewing machine set to a narrow zigzag stitch to finish raw edges.

Step 1 Begin by pinning and sewing the front pieces to the back at the shoulders. Then sew the sleeves to the armholes. In one continuous seam, sew the underarm and side seam so that the armholes align. Finish the raw edges with a serger, or zigzag stitch the seam allowances together.

Step 2 Finish the center front openings and neckline with a serger overlock stitch or machine zigzag. Take care not to pull the sweater as it goes through the serger or sewing machine.

Step 3 Lay out your trims, appliqué fabric, and embroidery thread, and select which you want to use. Fold under the ends of the trim and hand sew them to the front edges with a small running stitch (page 24). On the right side, extend the trim at the neckline into a small buttonhole loop and tack it in place (make sure the button fits through it). Hand sew the neckline trim the same way; remember to fold under the ends and stitch them to the sweater to prevent raveling.

Step 4 Cut bird, flower, or heart appliqués from felt or sweater remnants. Use the bird pattern and draw the flower and heart freehand. Hand sew them in place with a large running stitch and contrast embroidery thread.

Step 5 Sew the button opposite the trim loop. You might want to add a clothing label that indicates the sweater should only be dry cleaned.

Enjoy your little one-of-a-kind sweater and be ready for lots of compliments!

Hippie Chicks

These Hippie Chicks look ready to sing and brighten your day. They're all about peace, love, and happiness, and they like hanging out and listening to music. They are made from a white angora and wool blend sweater that was randomly hand painted in sunny and psychedelic colors. A fuzzy texture, such as mohair or angora, and a light color will yield the best results. Sunshine was made from an unfelted sweater, whereas Opal was made from a sweater that was felted after it was painted.

Getting Started

With the exception of felting, the construction for both is identical. If you choose to use a felted sweater, you can felt before or after the dye process. Felting after the dye process yields a smoother and more interesting color blend. Take necessary safety precautions when working with dyes, and follow the manufacturer's instructions.

Prepare and mix the dyes. Put enough hot water to cover the fabric and 1 to 2 teaspoons of citric acid or vinegar (to prevent the dye from running) in a wide nonreactive pan. Place the sweater fabric right side up in the dye pan. Paint the sweater by dabbing drops of dye wherever you want color. Before the color absorbs into the fabric, lightly tap the area with a spoon or paintbrush to disperse and mottle the color. Once you like the look of the

fabric and the water is clear, remove the sweater carefully and lay it flat to dry.

Blocking: After the fabric is painted, felt (page 12) it if you want, then block (page 11) fabric flat and let it dry.

Cutting out the pattern pieces: The pattern pieces for Opal are slightly smaller because she is made with felted fabric. With the wrong side of the dried fabric facing up, trace around the

body of the chick with a fabric-marking pen. Flip the pattern over and trace the body again. Trace the wing pattern twice on the wrong side of the fabric, then flip the wing pattern over and trace two more wings. Before cutting, check to see that the two body pieces and four wing pieces (two each) are mirror images. Trace and cut one beak piece from felt or contrast fabric.

Step 1 With right sides facing, sandwich the beak between the two body layers, as shown by the dashed lines on the pattern. Sew around the chick bodies with a ⅜" (1 cm) seam allowance, making sure to leave the seam open on the bottom between the two dots. Because the fabric is stretchy, there is no need to clip the curves. Turn the chick right side out and stuff it with polyester fiberfill.

Step 2 With the right sides of two mirror-image wing pieces together, sew around the wing, leaving the seam open between the dashes. Turn the wing right side out and stuff very lightly with the fiberfill. Hand sew the opening closed. Repeat with the remaining wing pieces.

Step 3 Refer to the dashed lines within the pattern as reference for wing placement. Hand sew the wider edge of the wings to the body so they flare out slightly, to give the chicks depth and dimension.

Step 4 Slip stitch the bottom opening of the chick closed. Repeat instructions to sew multiple chicks.

Materials

- felted sweater fabric in different colors or patterns
- cotton print fabric remnants in different patterns
- several colors of embroidery floss
- polyester fiberfill
- two 1" (2.5 cm)-diameter buttons or plastic animal eyes with locking backs
- small scraps of felted wool or craft felt in assorted colors
- ½ yard (45.7 cm) of 1" (2.5 cm)-wide ruffled eyelet trim, lace, ribbon, or other decorative trim

Tools

- basic tool kit (page 15)
- patterns (page 153)
- iron and ironing board

Woolie Minkie & Woolie Piggie

These two charming, handmade stuffed animals have a recycled pedigree and personality plus. Turn a favorite old sweater and colorful scraps of fabric into a loveable friend for someone you know. These projects use straightforward machine sewing, basic hand stitching, fabrics, stuffing, buttons, and other trims to create a one-of-a-kind work of art.

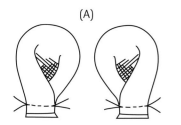

(A)

Getting Started

Enlarge the patterns 200 percent. Use a ¼" (6 mm) seam allowance for all seams. Backstitch at the beginning and end of all seams. Trace around the pattern pieces on the wrong side of the fabric with a fabric-marking pen and cut out the pieces as follows:

From different colors of felted wool: one head, one body, two ears, two feet

From different patterns of cotton remnants: one head, one body, two ears, two feet

From scraps of felted wool or craft felt: two hats

Step 1 Pin one wool ear to one cotton ear with the right sides together, leaving the lower edge open. Machine sew the seam with small stitches. Trim the seam and turn the ear right side out. Fold the open end to create ear shape as shown in diagram A. Stitch across the lower edge. Repeat with the remaining two ears.

Step 2 Pin and sew the lower edge of the felted fabric head to the top of the cotton fabric body with the right sides together. Pin and sew the lower edge of the cotton fabric head to the top of the felted fabric body with the right sides together. Press the seams open with an iron.

DESIGNED BY SARAH STEEDMAN

(B)

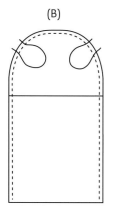

(C)

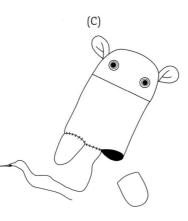

(D)

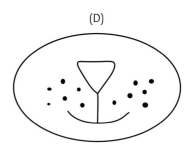

Step 3 Pin the sides and top of these newly joined pieces with the right sides together, matching seams. Insert the ears between the pieces in the curves of the head as shown (see diagram B). Make sure the ears are positioned inward with the cotton print facing the wool head in between the fabric layers.

Sew the head and body together (leave the bottom open for turning). Trim the seam allowance. Turn the head/body right side out. Check to make sure the seams are tight. If they aren't, turn it inside out and restitch.

Step 4 Pin and sew two feet pieces with the wrong sides together, close to the cut edge, so the seam is visible from the right side. Leave the top edge open. Repeat with remaining feet pieces.

Step 5 Sew the button eyes or attach the animal eyes before stuffing the body. Place a small circle of felt under each eye to

add depth to the face. Firmly stuff the body and feet with small handfuls of stuffing.

Step 6 Finger press the bottom edge of the body 1" (2.5 cm) to the inside. Insert the first foot 1" (2.5 cm) into the body. Using embroidery floss and embroidery needle, hand stitch the foot with small, even stitches as shown (see diagram C). Tuck the second foot in the other corner the same way and finish sewing the body closed. Knot the thread securely.

Step 7 Cut a 2" (5.1 cm)-oval and a ½" (1.3 cm)-triangle from felted wool or craft felt. Sew the triangle onto the oval with small stitches. Sew the mouth lines with straight stitches and the freckles with small straight stitches in contrast color embroidery floss (see diagram D). Sew the oval onto the face with small stitches as shown.

Step 8 Sew the hat pieces with the right sides together. Turn the hat right side out and stuff it.

Hand sew the bottom edge of the hat to the top of the head. Attach a ruffled eyelet collar and any other personal touches. Congratulations! You have finished your first Woolie Minkie!

Materials

- felted sweater fabric in 2 different colors
- printed cotton fabric remnant
- small scraps of felted wool or craft felt
- embroidery floss
- 15" (38.1 cm) lace or ruffled eyelet trim
- polyester fiberfill
- two ¼" (6 mm)-diameter buttons for eyes (optional)
- small flower appliqué (optional)

Tools

- basic tool kit (page 15)
- patterns (page 154)
- iron and ironing board

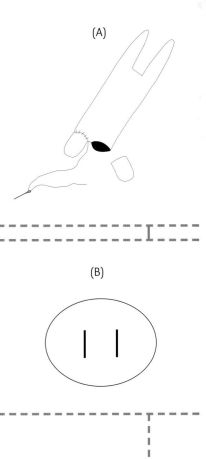

Woolie Piggie

Getting Started

Enlarge the patterns 200 percent. Use ¼" (6 mm) seam allowance for all seams. Backstitch at the beginning and end of all seams. Trace around the pattern pieces on the wrong side of the fabric with a fabric-marking pen and cut out the pieces as follows:

From different colors of felted wool:

- one body and two feet

From cotton remnant:

- one body

Step 1 Pin and sew the felted fabric body to cotton print body with the right sides together, leaving the lower edge open. Turn the body right side out and press it flat with the iron. Fold the bottom edge of the body 1" (2.5 cm) to the inside and press.

Step 2 Pin and sew the feet pieces with the wrong sides together, leaving the top edges open. The seam will be visible on the right side.

Step 3 Stuff the body (but not the ears) and the feet. With embroidery floss and an embroidery needle, hand stitch the feet to the body so they extend ½ to 1" (1.3 to 2.5 cm) into the body cavity. Sew around each foot and the small opening between the feet as shown. Knot the thread securely (see diagram A).

Step 4 Fold the ears down over the front of the head and tack them in place on each side of the ear. Sew buttons for eyes, or use black embroidery floss and straight stitches for the eyes. Use the same black embroidery floss for the mouth.

Step 5 Cut a 1" (2.5 cm)-diameter circle of felt for the nose and embroider two straight lines in the center as shown (see diagram B). Sew the nose to the face between the eyes. Sew the mouth with small backstitches (see page 23). Add a piece of ruffled eyelet around the low waist for a skirt, a flower appliqué near the ear, and your own personal touches.

Congratulations! You have finished your first Woolie Piggie!

(A)

(B)

Hoot-Toot the Owl

What could be wiser than turning two colorful sweaters into a friendly looking owl? Keep him perched on your desk or near your bed to help you answer all your questions. Make his front section from a soft angora or cashmere sweater and rub him for good luck and quick advice!

Materials

- 2 different-colored felted sweater fabrics for owl body
- yellow and black craft felt or felted sweater fabric remnants for feet, beak, and eyes
- black embroidery floss
- matching sewing thread for each fabric color
- polyester fiberfill stuffing
- 24-gauge floral wire

Tools

- basic tool kit (page 15)
- patterns (page 155)

Getting Started

Enlarge the patterns 200 percent. Backstitch at the beginning and end of all seams. Fold the fabric in half with the right sides together to cut any patterns that need to be cut twice. Trace around the pattern pieces on the wrong side of the fabric with a fabric-marking pen, and cut out the pieces as follows:

From first owl body color: owl body (cut two), owl wings (cut two sets for a total of four), tuft or ear (cut two), and head gusset (cut one)

From second owl body color: owl body gusset (cut one), owl eye bottom (cut two)

From yellow felt or felted sweater: owl beak (cut two), owl foot (cut two sets for a total of four), owl eye top (cut two)

From black felt or felted sweater: owl eye middle (cut two)

Step 1 Pin and sew the head gusset and body gusset with the right sides together along the edge marked "A." Trim the seam close to the stitching.

Step 2 Pin and sew one body to the combined gussets so that the right sides are together and the location on the body marked "A" is aligned with the seam sewn in step 1, the end of the head gusset lines up with the "B," and the end of the body gusset lines up with "C," as marked on the owl body pattern. Trim the seam.

Step 3 Repeat with the remaining body piece, except leave a 1" (2.5 cm) opening along the owl's back for stuffing.

Step 4 Turn the owl right side out and stuff it firmly. Shape the head by using small bits of fiberfill and shaping it with your hands. Slip stitch (page 25) the opening closed.

Step 5 Whipstitch (page 25) the bottom eye pieces onto the head and the top eye pieces to the middle pieces. With black embroidery thread, take three or four straight stitches across the center of the top eye pieces. Whipstitch the middle eye pieces to the bottom eye pieces, as shown in the photograph.

Step 6 Create the tufts by folding the points marked "D" together. Hand sew the opening between the points closed. Repeat for second tuft. Pin each tuft to the side of the head near the gusset seam, so that the tufts open away from the head, and whipstitch them in place.

Step 7 Create the beak by whipstitching the two pieces together, except along the back. Stuff the beak firmly through the opening. Pin the beak to the owl's face between the eyes and whipstitch in place with yellow thread to match the beak.

Step 8 Create two wings by pinning and machine sewing two wing pieces with the wrong sides together. Trim the seam close to the stitching. Pin the wings into place on the body, and whipstitch the top curve of the wing.

Step 9 Create the feet by whipstitching two feet pieces, with the wrong sides together, along all the edges except for the back. Fold and shape floral wire into the foot shape and insert it in the opening. Whipstitch the opening closed and then the feet to the owl body. Shape and curve the talons.

tip

Matching the thread color to the sweater fabric helps the hand stitches blend in better.

Materials

- felted sweater for flower
- felted sweater for design and details
- felted sweater for leaves

Tools

- scissors
- pins
- felting needles and mat patterns (page 147)

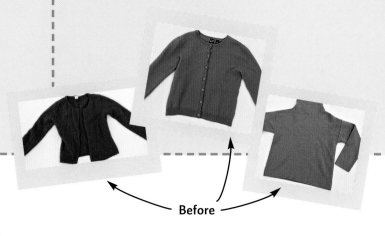

Before

Bloomin' Place Mats

Add a splash of color to your table with these oversized blooming beauties. With a snip of the scissors and a poke of the needle, you'll be on your way to a field of flowered place mats.

tip

Use a toothpick to hold the little pieces in place until they are secure.

Getting Started

Enlarge the patterns 400 percent on a photocopy machine, or draw your own similarly shaped patterns. Cut out all the pattern pieces. Pin the patterns on the desired color felted sweaters and cut out the shapes.

Step 1 Lay the petal accents or designs along the edges (if desired) and in the center of the flower, as the pattern indicates. Needle felt the design pieces in place (see page 12). Trim away the excess fabric if necessary, for clean edges.

Step 2 Pin the leaves, as the pattern indicates, so they underlap the flower base by 1 to 2" (2.5 to 5.1 cm). Needle felt each leaf in place and trim away the extra fabric for neat edges.

Nine-to-Five Magazine File Cozy

Add a little pizzazz to your office with a funky magazine file cozy. It's the perfect cover-up for those unattractive but functional cardboard and plastic magazine files. "Nine to Five" is made from scraps of felted sweaters that have been left over from other projects. You can use other fabrics, especially ones with interesting texture, as well.

tip

Paper grocery bags are great for pattern drafting.

Getting Started

Trace onto craft paper each side of the magazine file that you intend to cover, to create your patterns. Pieces include: side one, side two, front spine, back spine, and bottom. Add a ¼" (6 mm) seam allowance around each piece and label accordingly. Trace all the patterns, except the bottom piece, onto the lining fabric and interfacing. Trace the bottom piece onto lining fabric only. Cut out all the pieces of lining and interfacing.

Step 1 Set the lining and interfacing fabric pieces aside. On the side and spine patterns, draw random curved lines. Keep the lines smooth and minimize sharp corners or curves to create soft patchwork shapes. It helps to use a flexible ruler.

Step 2 On the paper pattern, number or label each shape and then cut the shapes apart. Trace your patchwork-shape designs onto the corresponding interfacing pieces to help keep track of the desired positioning. Use these patterns to cut out pieces of felted sweaters.

Step 3 Place the shaped sweater pieces on the corresponding piece of interfacing so that all the pieces meet. Zigzag-stitch the pieces together, stitching through the interfacing. Set your sewing machine so the zigzag stitch is wide enough that it joins the sweater pieces. Stitch both side pieces and both spine pieces.

Step 4 With the wrong sides together (so the seams are visible), stitch the sides to the spines so they take the shape of the magazine file. Sew the

DESIGNED BY ANNE KUO LUKITO

bottom lining to the lower edge of the joined pieces with a straight machine stitch, close to the fabric edges. With the right sides together, stitch the side and spine lining pieces together in the same manner.

Step 5 With the wrong sides together, stitch the lining to the interfacing side of the felted sweater pieces, close to the fabric edges, with a straight machine stitch at the top edge only. Insert the magazine holder into the cozy and tuck the lining to the inside. The magazine file is now sandwiched between the sweater-interfacing layer and the lining layer.

Materials for Superstar Pillow
· felted sweater with center motif
· coordinating felted sweater
· coordinating embroidery floss and matching sewing thread
· batting

Tools
· basic tool kit (page 15)
· ruler, paper, and pencil
· plate or circular object the size of desired pillow
· scissors
· straight pins
· embroidery needle

Before

Sophisticated Pillow Collection

When you're looking to spice up your space, nothing is easier then whipping up a few new throw pillows or re-covering old ones. Gather a few sweaters that are complementary in color and texture, and give them new life in a couture-style pillow collection. Incorporate existing features, such as the star motif on this round pillow, the nubby texture of the ring and classic square pillows, and the plaid pattern of the bolster, into your pillow design.

tip

Cut a window in the circle pattern so it is easier to center the motif. Fold the circle pattern in half and then in half again. This creates a wedge shape like a slice of pie. Cut off the point of the pie shape to open the center and retain the shape of the pattern.

For the Superstar Pillow:

Step 1 Make a paper pattern by tracing around a plate or circular object that is the desired pillow size. Cut one circle from the front of the sweater with the motif in the center, and a second circle from the back of the sweater.

Step 2 Measure the circumference of the pillow front and back. Cut strips from the coordinating sweater 4" (10.2 cm)

wide and as long as the pillow circumference plus 1" (2.5 cm) for the seam allowance. If necessary, sew two or more strips together to obtain the desired length to make the pillow side.

Step 3 Fold the side in half and in half again, and mark each quarter with a pin. Use pins to mark the four quarters of the circle piece. With the wrong sides together, align the pin markings of the side and

front pillow pieces. Use extra pins to secure the two pieces evenly. Blanket stitch (page 24) to join the pieces.

Step 4 Cut circles of batting and position them under the pillow front. Add enough batting to form the pillow. Pin the back and side together as in step 3 and blanket stitch in place.

Before

Tubular Pillow

For the Tubular Pillow:

Step 1 Measure the length, circumference, and radius of the bolster form. Cut the fabric the following size:

width-circumference + 1"
length-radius + length + radius + 1"

tip

If you have batting readily available, roll it up to make your own (any size) pillow bolster form.

If there is any central motif, be sure to center it.

Step 2 Fold the piece widthwise with the right sides together. Sew the seam with a ½" (1.3 cm) seam allowance, to form a tube.

Step 3 Turn the fabric right side out and slide and center the pillow form inside.

Step 4 With heavy-duty thread, hand sew a large running stitch close to the ends of the fabric tube. Pull the threads to gather the ends.

Step 5 Cover the button blanks with coordinating scraps of felted sweater fabric, following the instructions on the package.

Step 6 Thread the long upholstery needle with a length of string that is twice as long as the pillow. Knot one of the buttons onto the ends of the string. Insert the needle into the center of one end of the pillow, through the pillow and out the opposite end.

Cut the string off the needle and tie the other button onto the ends. Before you knot the string, pull it taut so the buttons sink into the pillow. Knot the string securely and trim away the excess.

Materials for Sooooo Square Pillow
- sweater
- square pillow form

Tools
- basic tool kit (page 15)

Before

Soooooo Square Pillow

For the Square Pillow:

Step 1 Cut two squares from the front and back of the sweater. The size of the squares determines the size of the pillow form. If a standard-size pillow form doesn't work, adjust the size of the squares or use batting instead. Pin the two squares with the right sides together and sew. Leave half of one side open. Turn the pillow right side out and fill it with the pillow form (or batting). Fold the seam allowance to the inside and slip stitch (page 25) the pillow closed.

Before

Oh! Pillow

For the Oh! Pillow:

Step 1 Cut the sleeves off of the sweater, perpendicular to the top fold of the sleeve (see diagram A). If there are cuffs, cut them off. Turn one sleeve inside out and slip the remaining sleeve inside it so that right sides are together and the cut edges align. Pin and sew together the cut edges at one end of the sleeves.

Step 2 Pull the inner sleeve out to form one long tube with the wrong side out. If the sleeves were tapered, straighten the tube by marking a new stitching line, so that the tube is the same width the entire length (see diagram B). Sew a new seam and trim off the excess fabric.

Step 3 With the heavy-duty thread, sew a large running stitch (page 24) in the seam allowance just next to the seam. Turn the tube right side out and pull the thread to gather the tube into a circle. Fill the tube with batting and slip stitch (page 25) the tube closed.

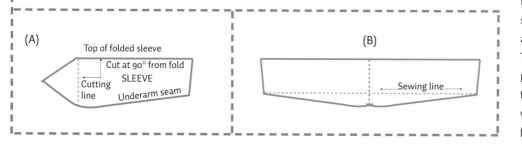

(A)   Top of folded sleeve
Cut at 90° from fold
SLEEVE
Cutting line   Underarm seam

(B)   Sewing line

DESIGNED BY MARTHA BISHOP

Materials

· 2 or 3 felted sweaters
  in different colors or patterns
· 3" (7.6 cm) of ¼" (6 mm)-diameter
  cotton cording for each pot
  holder's hanging loop
· matching sewing thread

Tools

· sewing machine
· scissors or rotary cutter
  and cutting mat
· straight pins
· ruler

Piles o' Pot Holders

These easy-to-make, useful, colorful, and inexpensive pot
holders make great gifts. Everyone can use a new pot holder
and they are lightweight; perfect for mailing to friends and
relations who live far away. They machine wash beautifully
and should be hung on the line to dry.

Getting Started
For each pot holder, cut:
two different 8" (20.3 cm)
squares of felted sweater fabric
one 6 to 7" (15.2 to 17.8 cm)
circle in another color one 3"
(7.6 cm) length of cording.

Step 1 Pin the two squares
with the wrong sides together.
Fold the cording in half and tuck
the ends between the fabric layers at one of the corners to form
the hanging loop.

Step 2 Machine stitch ¼"
(6 mm) from the edge around
the perimeter of the pot holder.
Pivot at the corners and make
sure to catch the two cord ends
in the stitching. For added security, stitch over the previous
stitching at the corner with the
hanging loop.

Step 3 With the needle still
down, pivot the pot holder so
you can stitch toward the center. Position the felted circle in
the center and stitch toward it.

Sew around the outside
perimeter of the circle about
¼" (6 mm) from the edge.
Once you have sewn the circle
in place, start sewing in a spiral
pattern toward the center, turning the pot holder as you stitch.
Keep spiral stitches about ½"
(1.3 cm) apart. Once you reach
the center, take 2 or 3 backstitches and voilà, your pot
holder is ready!

Inspiration is the first step.

This section includes even more wonderful designs created by an amazing group of cut-ups from across the country. Take your inspiration from a whole project or a single element of something and transform it into your own design. The following pages are packed full of garments and accessories made with sweaters of all sorts of textures and colors that will have you running (not with scissors in your hand of course!) to your closets and drawers to see what old sweaters are waiting for a new life with just a few snips and stitches!

Sugar & Stripes & Everything Nice—The "Erika" Purse (Above) The construction of this purse is fairly basic, but the final look is anything but. Install the zipper between the two striped pieces to form the top of the purse. Insert a narrow strip of felted fabric in each of the slots at the lower edge of the handles and then stitch the strips to the top of the purse to attach the handles. Topstitch the remaining sides of the purse closed with a ¼" (6 mm) seam allowance.

DESIGNED BY KIM TAYLOR

The Cindy Purse

Unconventional gals need unconventional purses. One look at the bold diagonal stripes and avant-garde zipper placement, and it's clear that this purse isn't run of the mill. Mounted on the center front seam, the zipper provides unexpected yet easy entry to everything hidden inside. It's obvious that anyone who carries this purse has serious style.

The Joan Purse

Don't let the soft, creamy tones of this purse fool you. Underneath the demure exterior lies a rock-solid, versatile purse. The generous bucket shape gives plenty of room for essentials like a wallet and cell phone while still leaving room for a pair of vintage sunglasses and a paperback novel. Plus, the handles are the perfect size to carry the purse draped across your arm or slung over your shoulder.

DESIGNED BY MALKA DUBRAWSKY

Flower Mini Tote

This tote was made as a sample for a design class about crafting with recycled sweaters. The instructor never actually taught the students how to make the bag, because the class was for kids and the bag was a little too complicated for them. Nevertheless, the bag is a winning combination of materials and embroidery techniques. Notice how the "eye" bead brings the appliquéd flower to life.

BOTH PROJECTS DESIGNED BY MALKA DUBRAWSKY

iPod Cozy Necklace and The "Hand" Bag

iPod Cozy Necklace Many teenagers and adults alike are obsessed with their iPods and MP3 players. This iPod cozy design allows you to change selections and view your screen while your music maker is on. It even functions as a necklace with its multicolor beads and embroidery. **The "hand" bag** was inspired by a collection of *hamsas*, which are Mediterranean good-luck symbols. The hamsa is usually an upright or inverted hand with an eye in the center of the palm. This "eye" is a repurposed button. Below the hand are two buttons with Hebrew letters that spell the word *yad*, or "hand," in Hebrew.

DESIGNED BY STEFANIE GIRARD

Laptop Cozy

High tech meets low tech with this snuggly laptop cozy. Simply
felt a sweater vest down to the size of your laptop. This is easily
done by blocking it with a laptop-size piece of cardboard wrapped
in a plastic bag. Once the vest is the right size, stitch across the
bottom to close it up, and cut open the shoulder seams. Sew a button on the back of each
shoulder and cut aligning buttonholes on the front. Insert your computer and button it snug!

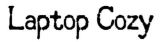

Before

Before

DESIGNED BY STEFANIE GIRARD

Sweater with Sassy New Sleeves

Whether you have worn out the elbows of your favorite sweater or are merely looking to spice things up, this novelty sleeve is so easy. All you need is a long-sleeved sweater, thread, and fabric bands (or even remnants) from another sweater. Draw two parallel lines across the middle of the sleeve as far apart as you want. Cut along the marked lines and use this piece as a pattern to cut the sleeve bands from the remaining accent sweater or fabric. Pin a band to the top and bottom of one sleeve and machine stitch it in place. Repeat for the other sleeve and you're off! Try making sleeves longer or shorter by adjusting the length of the new section!

Before

DESIGNED BY STEFANIE GIRARD

Pet Rock Sweater

Pet rocks are a blast from the past; this one gets a modern and cozy turtleneck sweater. All it takes is a few snips and stitches. Cut a front and back panel so they fit snuggly around the rock. Make two little sleeves and stitch them into the side seams. Make a small tube for the turtleneck and stitch it to the top of the body of the sweater. Hem the lower edge and slip it on your favorite pet rock.

DESIGNED BY STEFANIE GIRARD

Before

Beer Sweater

Who doesn't want to keep their drink from getting warm or their hands from getting cold as they grasp a refreshing bottled beverage? Cut two T-shaped pieces from a ribbed sweater and save a piece of the rib for the fold-over turtleneck. Hand or machine sew the pieces into a stylin' mini turtleneck sweater that does double duty!

Before

DESIGNED BY STEFANIE GIRARD

Blue Jumper

Transform a big, baggy sweater into a shapely jumper. All you have to do is cut off the sleeves and try the sweater on inside out. Pin it into a more fitted shape and machine stitch the new side seams and armholes. Add cute little patch pockets and voilà, you have a trendy new top for out and about.

DESIGNED BY STEFANIE GIRARD

Ruffles & Lace Scarf

Lace patterns are beautiful but a true challenge to knit. Pick a vertical area of the sweater and machine stitch to mark the desired edges of the scarf. Cut just outside the stitching. Cut as many strips as necessary to make the scarf the desired length. Sew the ends together to create one long scarf, with the finished sweater edges at each end of the scarf. Whipstitch (page 25) with yarn around the edges of the scarf. Weave two lengths of yarn through the center of the scarf and pull them to create the ruffled effect. Tie the yarns in a bow at each end to secure them.

Before

Before

DESIGNED BY STEFANIE GIRARD

Spot-on Messenger Bag

A striped and a solid-color wool sweater combine to make a super-sporty and soft messenger bag. This bag utilizes the shoulder seams and the long sleeves of the striped sweater to make the sides of the bag, and the solid sweater to make the flap. Cut a few remnants from the striped sweater into various size circles and needle felt (page 12) them to the flap to jazz it up.

DESIGNED BY STEFANIE GIRARD

Sassy Striped Pet Bed

We love to snuggle up in a sweater, so why not give our little pet friends
some sweater snuggle action? Convert the arms of a sweater into the
sides of the bed and the body of the sweater into the base. Stuff the bottom
with foam and the sides with batting, and your little one will be snoozing in comfort.

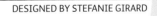

Before

DESIGNED BY STEFANIE GIRARD

Super-Sized Shrug

Thick and chunky knits offer intriguing design options. Separate the arms from the sweater and then reconnect them by lacing them with a bit of reclaimed yarn (page 19) from the body of the sweater...just like lacing up a shoe! Keep the shrug closed with a beautiful, bold button that will fit through a stitch in the knitting.

Before

DESIGNED BY STEFANIE GIRARD

Striped Vases

Do you want to turn a group of miss-matched vases into a vibrant, show-stopping collection? Raid your closet for a ribbed sweater with a bold color palette. With a few snips and stitches you'll certainly have a great conversation starter with a matched set of sweater-wearing vases!

Before

DESIGNED BY STEFANIE GIRARD

Fun Fair Isle Purse

It's hard to retire a favorite sweater, even when it doesn't work in your wardrobe. Don't pack it away; turn it into a cool new accessory. This purse uses the classic yoked Fair Isle pattern as the focal design feature. Slide coordinating beads onto beadable purse handle and you're sure to be stylin'!

Before

Before

DESIGNED BY STEFANIE GIRARD

Lacy Below The Waist

Update and convert a big oversized sweater from the past into a soft and comfortable skirt of any length. Cut the sweater below the sleeves and run elastic across the top to hold it up! Create extra shaping and style by running stretch ribbon through the sweater just above the hem, and tie it in a bow.

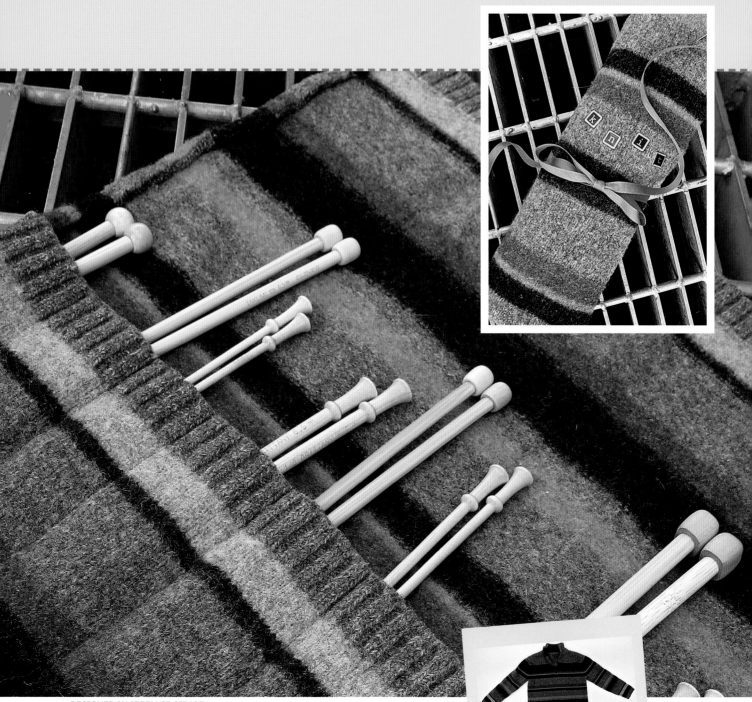

DESIGNED BY STEFANIE GIRARD

Before

Cozy Knitting Needle Case

All knitters need a place to store their needles; why not whip up a cute needle case from an old sweater to keep them safe and orderly. Cut the sweater so the bottom waist edge becomes the top of the pocket and the edge of the top flap. Sew several straight vertical lines to create long, thin pockets. A bit of ribbon keeps it closed and scrapbook letter brads add a quick personal touch.

Before

DESIGNED BY STEFANIE GIRARD

Knot Argyle Crop Sweater

Are you in love with the design on a sweater but not its size or shape? Grab your scissors and start cutting away! You be the designer. Simply slice the center, leaving two long tails to make a tie closure, and take a bit off the back for a cropped top. Fold under the cut edges and stitch to secure. Now, you have a cute, cropped tie sweater.

DESIGNED BY STEFANIE GIRARD

Awesome Embroidered Bag

Do you love details and unique features, but not taking on big projects? Here's the solution. Start with a sweater that's packed with great details and use them. Find an embroidered cardigan and a bit of ribbon and you'll put together a bag that looks like it took hours to make! Position the existing vertical button closure as the top closure for the bag and sew up the sides. Add a peekaboo detail to the strap by weaving a coordinating ribbon through it.

Before

DESIGNED BY STEFANIE GIRARD

Kick-A$$ Socks

Why not make something fun for below the knees? Have you got a ribbed sweater that has had a bit of misfortune? Recycle the sleeves into a fun pair of kneesocks. Cut the sleeves off and stitch them closed to form the toe seam. If your socks are bit baggy, take them in along the existing seam, especially at the ankles.

Before

DESIGNED BY STEFANIE GIRARD

Easy Envelope Clutch

A clutch purse is perfect when you need to carry only a
few little things. Why not make one out of a sweater with
a subtle print and accent it with a bold button. You can
whip up this project in less time than it will take you to get dressed!

Before

Before

DESIGNED BY STEFANIE GIRARD

Sporty Argyle Purse

Do you want to use a motif from a nonfelted sweater on a project that's made from a felted sweater? Simply use double-sided fusible web to adhere the nonfelted sweater to the felted one, and you're off and running! If you think the bag looks a little bare, look to the existing design elements. In this purse, the V shape of the knit stitches inspired a V-stitch embroidery pattern on the handle.

DESIGNED BY STEFANIE GIRARD

Before

Big Brown Bag

We all love to be prepared for everything, so a big bag is often a necessity! Use the ribbed bottom edge of the sweater. Flip it upside down and use it as a casing to enclose a big wooden circle purse handle. The stripe that spanned the chest area of the sweater now decorates the bottom of the bag.

Before

DESIGNED BY STEFANIE GIRARD

Stylin' Wide, Groovy Green, Stud-ly Blue Belts

Stylin' Wide Belt: Accessories often make an outfit and are some of the quickest and most fun projects to create. A wide belt with a big buckle gathers in a loose shirt or jazzes up a cute dress. Cut a piece of felted sweater, sew a few pieces together to get the right length, and sew a buckle at one end. Make lots of belts from all your leftover sweater scraps! **Groovy Green Belt:** How about recycling an old belt buckle along with your sweaters! Cut sweater strips from felted sweaters (piece them if you need to, for length) and attach an old or new buckle. If the belt seems flimsy, fuse stabilizer onto the back. **Stud-ly Blue Belt:** Belts can tie an outfit together or top off a pair of jeans with a splash of color. You can make a whole bunch of striped belts with a single striped sweater. Add embellishments, such as different size silver studs, to give the belt sparkle. Use D-rings to close the belt.

Before

DESIGNED BY STEFANIE GIRARD

Seeing Spots & Stripes Tissue Box Turtleneck Cozies

Are you looking for a way to dress up or disguise those necessary tissue boxes found everywhere about the house? Whether they're striped or spotted, simply snip the sleeves off old sweaters and slip them over the tissue box. Give the cuff a fold or two to create the turtleneck on top.

DESIGNED BY STEFANIE GIRARD

Before

Lace-It-Up Cable Sweater

So, you don't like to mess up your hair taking on and off a sweater? Why not cut a pullover sweater up the middle and turn it into a cardigan. Sew eyelet trim to the center front opening and run satin ribbon through the eyelet for a sexy, lace-up sweater. For a final touch, attach a few crocheted bobbles for a bit of whimsy.

DESIGNED BY STEFANIE GIRARD

Sweater Head Headband

Taming the locks can be a challenge! Why not dress up a plain headband with bold-print sweater fabric. Cut or piece enough strips so you have long ties to keep the wayward curls in place. Center the strip over the headband and glue the cut ends of the strip to the underside of the headband. Hand stitch the long tie ends with the raw edges folded under, to finish the look.

Before

Before

DESIGNED BY STEFANIE GIRARD

Biting-Edge Houndstooth Miniskirt

Sweaters are often more decorative in the front than the back. Even if the front is a little over the top, don't overlook the back. This wild floral front almost hides the awesome houndstooth pattern on the back of the sweater, which was boldly converted into a cute miniskirt with a kilt pin closure. The back of the sweater was cut into three panels and sewn into one rectangular piece. The sweater trim was cut off and resewn around the edges to finish the waist, sides, and hem.

DESIGNED BY JENNI PAGANO

Rings to Relish Sweater Bag

This purse was inspired by an advertising postcard from a favorite boutique. The color combination was fabulous and I just happened to have sweater felt in my stash to replicate the scheme! I laid the rings out on the fly, wrapping a few of the designs around the back. The large buttons are new—old stock from a button factory in Texas. I used yarn unraveled from yet another sweater to create a blanket stitch around the cut top edge of this bag.

DESIGNED BY LOUISE GOLDSMITH

Retro Hats

The Midnight in the City beret (above left): This black beret was inspired by a canceled trip to Paris. Nothing soothes the creative soul like kicking into gear and making something beautiful.

The Vizcaya hat (above center): This gray and blue pillbox hat was inspired by the formal Italian gardens at Vizcaya in Miami, Florida. The house and gardens are right on Biscayne Bay.

The Highland Fling hat (above right): This gray and plaid pillbox was made entirely from free fabric. The plaid came from the "stash bash" (folks bring fabric they no longer want) at our monthly ASG (American Sewing Guild) meeting.

DESIGNED BY JENNI PAGANO

Felt Rocks! Necklace

Nine different felted green and greenish sweaters combine with a serious bead collection to form the basis for this versatile loopable necklace.

DESIGNED BY JENNI PAGANO

Sweaters for the Desert Earrings

In Tucson, Arizona, wool sweaters are rarely needed, so many perfectly good sweaters can be found in thrift stores. These earrings are a creative way to recycle a beloved wardrobe item from another climate or get some more wear from a rogue sweater that slipped into the dryer. I've used snippets of yarn recycled from a silk sweater to sew them together. The yarn was dyed with Kool-Aid, but you could just as easily use embroidery floss! Finish with complementary beads

DESIGNED BY STEFANIE GIRARD

Everything-in-its-Place Mats

A pair of sporty striped place mats with a pocket for silverware will dress up your table indoors or out. Make a set for a housewarming gift; a new house can always use some creative touches.

DESIGNED BY ANNE KUO LUKITO

Shelly Tortoise

Shelly the tortoise likes to sit and lounge by a sunny window, basking in the solar heat. She makes a wonderful floor pillow for you and your family. Beware if you have pets—they will surely claim Shelly as their own. Everything about Shelly is recycled. Her outer shell is composed of felted sweaters cut into hexagonal pieces, while her bottom shell is made from leftover fabric. Shelly is even stuffed with scraps and remnants of sweater bits, as well as packing peanuts and polyester stuffing from an old pillow.

DESIGNED BY MINDY RELYEA

Twelve Days of Christmas Mittens & Stockings

A fun grouping of felted holiday stockings and mittens makes an adorable and useful holiday decoration. They're the perfect place to tuck mini gifts and notes to share throughout the holidays.

DESIGNED BY ANNE KUO LUKITO

Violet Flower Bag

Violet is the perfect, truly unique accessory for a fun, feminine girl. It's made from the sleeve of a wool sweater that was hand dyed and felted. The flap is actually the shoulder of the sleeve. The embroidered flower stem artfully hides the seam of the sleeve while providing design interest. Violet is finished with a button closure camouflaged by a flower, made from a hole-filled cashmere sweater.

DESIGNED BY ANNE KUO LUKITO

Gwlana Woven Hat & Cosmopolitan Hat

Gwyla Woven Hat: This funky hat is woven from strips of felted sweaters. Ribbed sweaters make a comfortable-fitting hat. Turn the hat over and you have a bowl, ideal for holding your roving, yarns or bits of felt. It also makes a grand conversation piece on your coffee table. Weaving strips from sweaters without ribbing will yield a sturdier bowl. **Cosmpolitan Hat:** This bold, beautiful cosmopolitan hat, inspired by the cloche hats worn by women in the 1920s and by actress Louise Brooks, is for the girl with confidence. Give it a custom-made touch by adding a lining.

DESIGNED BY ANNE KUO LUKITO

Snow & Ski Headbands

Named after the fuzzy angora sweater from which they are made, "Snow" and "Ski" are stylish head-bands that are super easy to make! Cut a 2" (5.1 cm)-wide strip of felted sweater fabric as long as necessary to fit around your head. **For "Snow,"** (center), cut a strip from a cable sweater. Make sure the strip has some of the cable detail in it. Sew the ends to form a loop. **For "Ski,"** (bottom right), weave two thin satin ribbons through the piece of felted sweater with a tapestry needle. Straight stitch across the headband to sew on the ribbbons. Use the ribbons to tie the headband in place.

DESIGNED BY TAWNY HOLT

The Sweetheart Top

Repurpose a soft cashmere sweater into a glamorous tank top. Use the sleeves to make a neckline ruffle, creating a hot new look.

DESIGNED BY TAWNY HOLT

Garden Tank

Combine a salvaged floral-patterned wool sweater with a layered appliqué and vintage fabric ruffle to make an adorable top, perfect for a spring day.

DESIGNED BY TAWNY HOLT

The Pirate Dress & The Merry Mod

The Pirate Dress (left) and **the Merry Mod** (right): Mix and match black-and-white wool and vintage fabrics in bold and demure stripes to make a cute pair of fun dresses.

DESIGNED BY TAWNY HOLT

The Vintage Modern Romper

This super-sporty romper is topped and hemmed with sections of an old wool sweater. The skirt that joins them is made from vintage fabric. It's perfect for a trip to the thrift store on a quest for more fabulous sweaters.

DESIGNED BY TAWNY HOLT

The Hopeless Romantic Top & The Garden Romper

The Hopeless Romantic Top: A lovely yellow wool sweater gets a new look with topstitched seams and appliquéd details. Once the sleeves are gone, the sweater looks like a breath of fresh summer air.

The Garden Romper: Rework an old cashmere top by adding a vintage fabric collar and skirt to make a delightful summer sundress!

DESIGNED BY TAWNY HOLT

The Breeze Top

Piece together the sleeves of felted wool sweaters to make a one-of-a-kind halter top. Use similar color sweaters, or a palette of bold colors; either way, the shape of the sleeves makes a wonderful, swing-shaped top!

DESIGNED BY MARTHA BISHOP

Circle & Square Pillows and Blanket

These blankets and pillows are so soft and warm, and why wouldn't they be? They're made from circles cut from old felted sweaters. The back of the pillows are made from the center front of a cardigan, so they button open and closed. Some of the circles have pockets for secret messages or the TV remote control!

DESIGNED BY AMANDA KRUEGER

Sweater Creatures

Theses little cuties are born from the sleeves of old felted sweaters. So young and small, they are hard to identify, but their wide eyes and big hearts will surely make you smile. Easy to sew and personalize, these creatures are fast and fun to make for gift giving (or to keep for yourself!). Add a cute ribbon collar with a tag for their name, and they will be yours forever. Note: Due to their wild and unpredictable nature, these creatures are not suited for babies under the age of three.

DESIGNED BY SUSAN BEAL

Sweater Sparkles Jewelry

These little accessories are fun to make and even more fun to wear! They're perfect for putting small sweater scraps from other projects to good use! And, with embellishments like a vintage button, a felt rosette, a fabric flower, or a little rickrack, you add a bit of sparkle to the mix. Make yourself a ring, brooch, or pendant—or a matching set—in all your favorite colors.

DESIGNED BY TAWNY HOLT

The Plum Swing Top

Sometimes, all you have to do is cut away the lower half of a sweater and give it a fabric ruffle, to create a new top that is full of excitement and energy. Add a floral appliqué from the wool you aren't using. Don't throw any wool away—save it for your next project!

DESIGNED BY LARISSA BROWN

Shrugette

When an adult sweater felts, it shrinks. Depending on the size of the sweater you start with, you can finish with a cute little shrug with scaled-down proportions to fit adult, teen, or child! This shrug is made from multiple sweaters pieced together with blanket stitch accents, perfect for any fashion maven.

DESIGNED BY L. K. LUDWIG

M Is for Monster

Monsters are cheery sorts, though by necessity quite solitary, except for the Christmas holidays, when they gather to sing carols. Monsters adore caroling, except they aren't very good at singing on key. That's where the trouble begins ... one monster begins to accuse another of being flat during "Jingle Bells" and then, you know, like your mom told you, "It's all fun and games until someone loses an eye." Just ask Mr. Monster, he'll tell you that it's so. Mr. Monster is made of fabrics from felted wool sweaters, and trimmed in bits of vintage buttons and velvet ribbon.

THE PATTERNS

A Bird in the Hand Purse

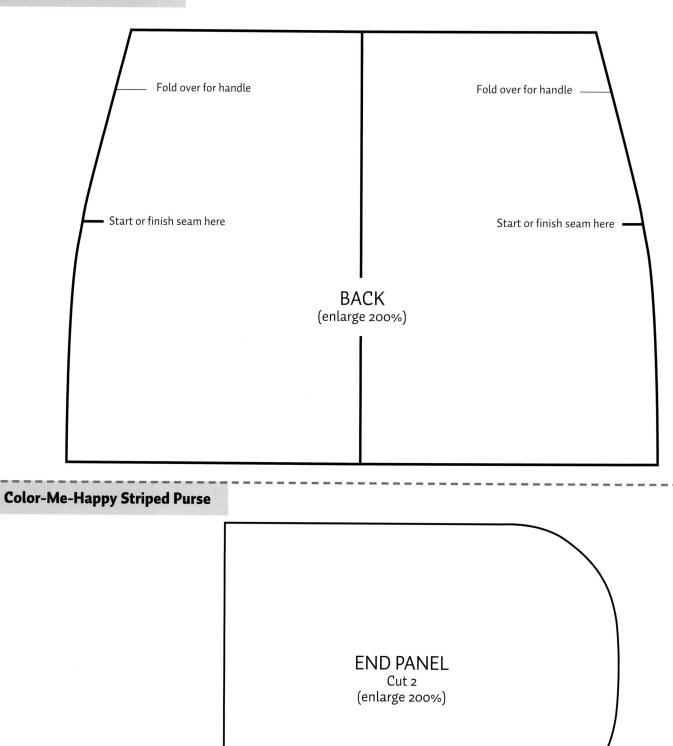

Fold over for handle

Fold over for handle

Start or finish seam here

Start or finish seam here

BACK
(enlarge 200%)

Color-Me-Happy Striped Purse

END PANEL
Cut 2
(enlarge 200%)

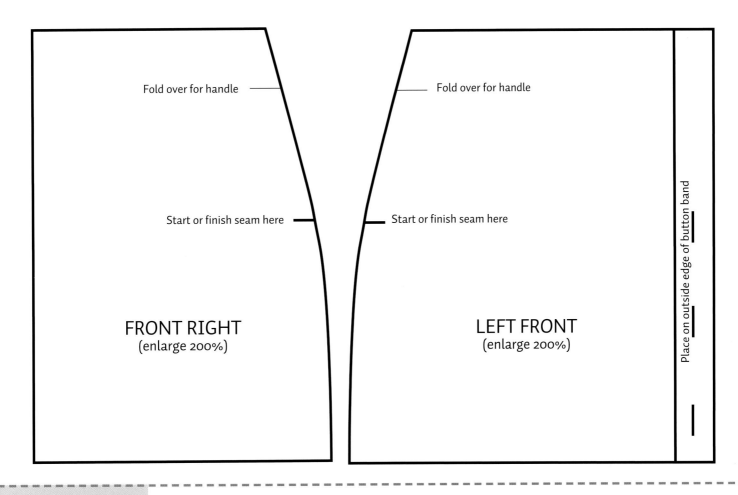

Fold over for handle

Fold over for handle

Start or finish seam here

Start or finish seam here

Place on outside edge of button band

FRONT RIGHT
(enlarge 200%)

LEFT FRONT
(enlarge 200%)

Limelight Purse

FLOWER TOP

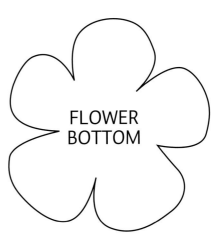

FLOWER
BOTTOM

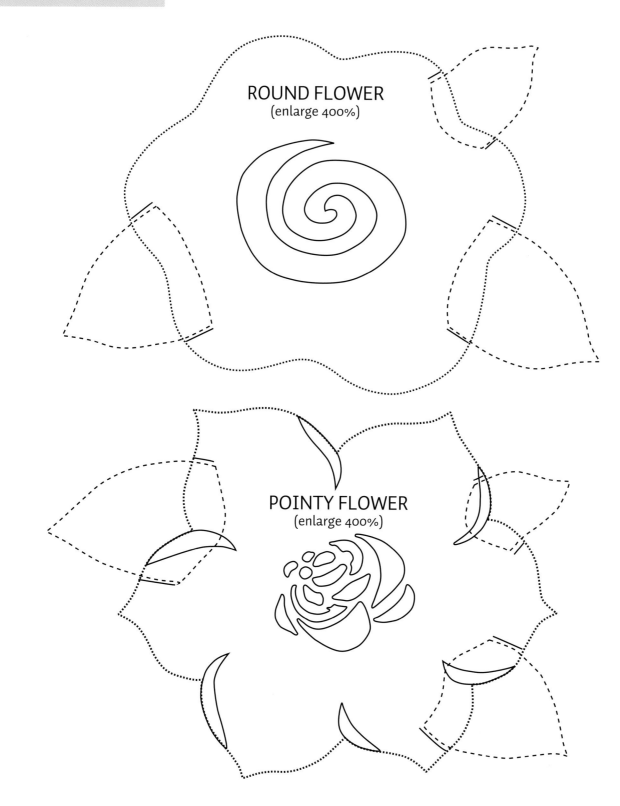

ROUND FLOWER
(enlarge 400%)

POINTY FLOWER
(enlarge 400%)

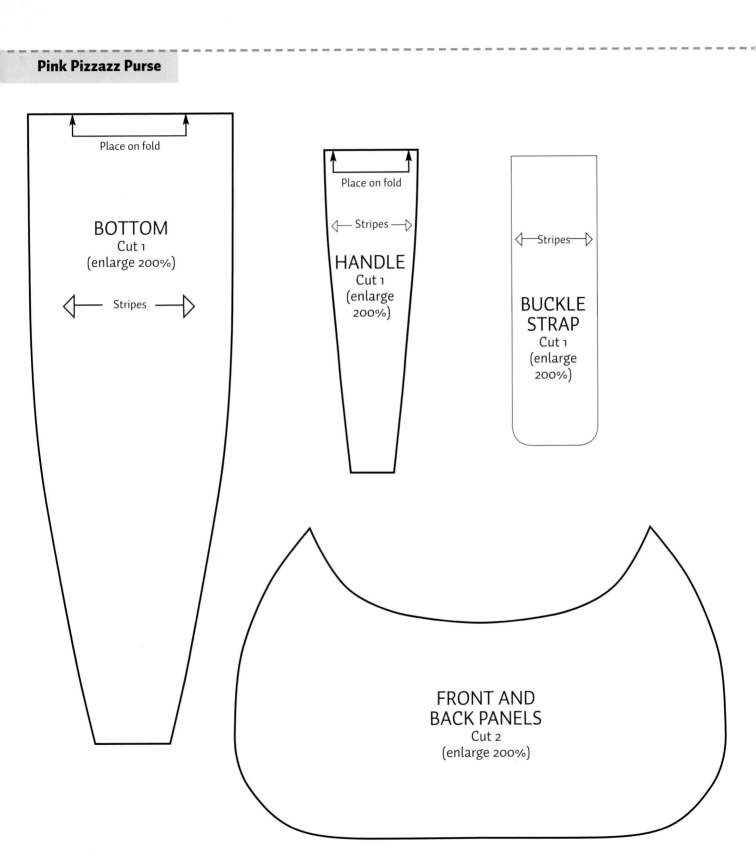

Place on fold

BOTTOM
Cut 1
(enlarge 200%)

←— Stripes —→

Place on fold

←— Stripes —→

HANDLE
Cut 1
(enlarge 200%)

←— Stripes —→

BUCKLE
STRAP
Cut 1
(enlarge 200%)

FRONT AND
BACK PANELS
Cut 2
(enlarge 200%)

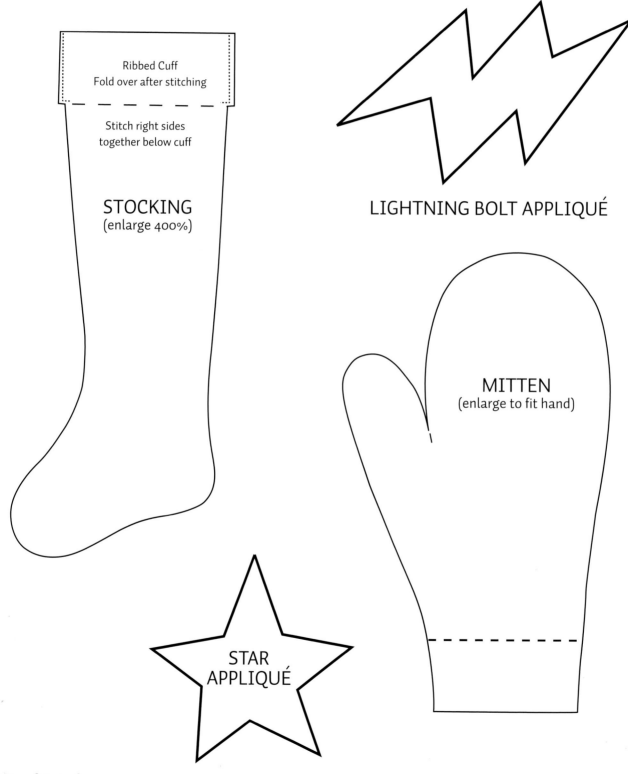

Ribbed Cuff
Fold over after stitching

Stitch right sides
together below cuff

STOCKING
(enlarge 400%)

LIGHTNING BOLT APPLIQUÉ

MITTEN
(enlarge to fit hand)

STAR
APPLIQUÉ

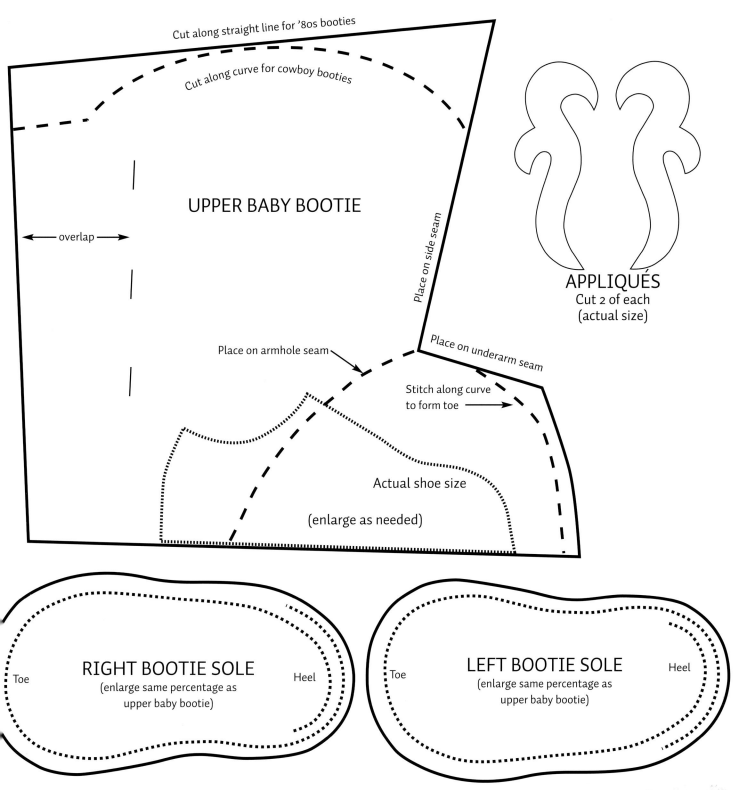

Cut along straight line for '80s booties

Cut along curve for cowboy booties

UPPER BABY BOOTIE

overlap

Place on side seam

APPLIQUÉS
Cut 2 of each
(actual size)

Place on armhole seam

Place on underarm seam

Stitch along curve
to form toe

Actual shoe size

(enlarge as needed)

RIGHT BOOTIE SOLE
(enlarge same percentage as
upper baby bootie)

Toe

Heel

LEFT BOOTIE SOLE
(enlarge same percentage as
upper baby bootie)

Toe

Heel

HEADBAND
Cut 1
(enlarge 200%)

Place on fold

Pom-pom Hat

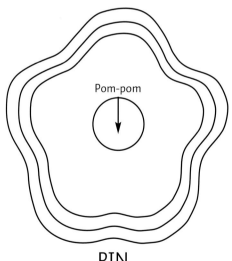

Pom-pom

PIN
Cut 1 flower of each size

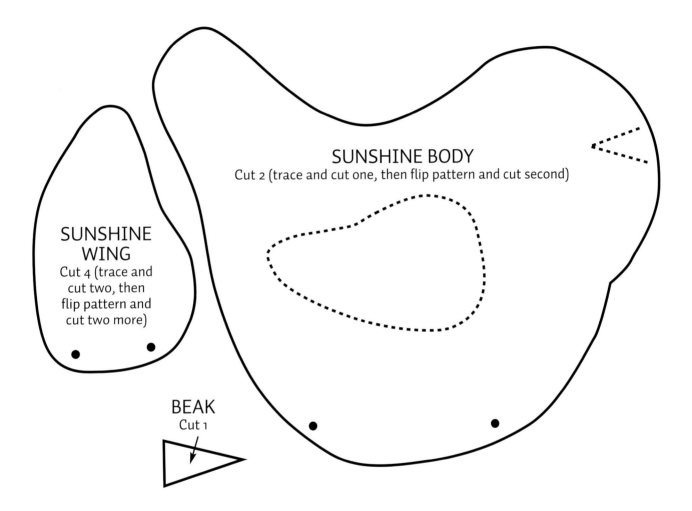

SUNSHINE BODY
Cut 2 (trace and cut one, then flip pattern and cut second)

SUNSHINE
WING
Cut 4 (trace and
cut two, then
flip pattern and
cut two more)

BEAK
Cut 1

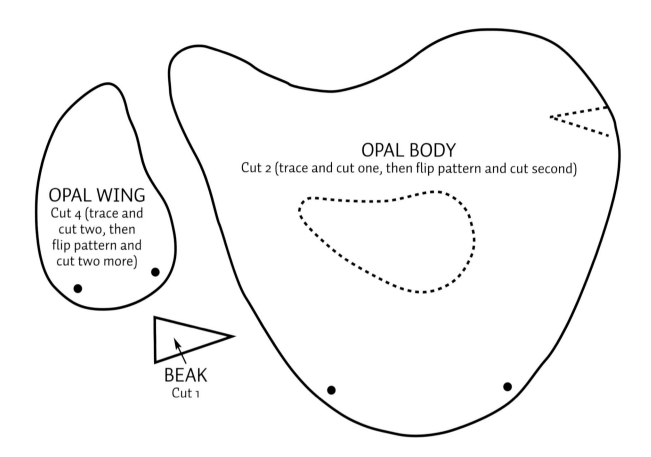

OPAL WING
Cut 4 (trace and
cut two, then
flip pattern and
cut two more)

OPAL BODY
Cut 2 (trace and cut one, then flip pattern and cut second)

BEAK
Cut 1

Woolie Minkie

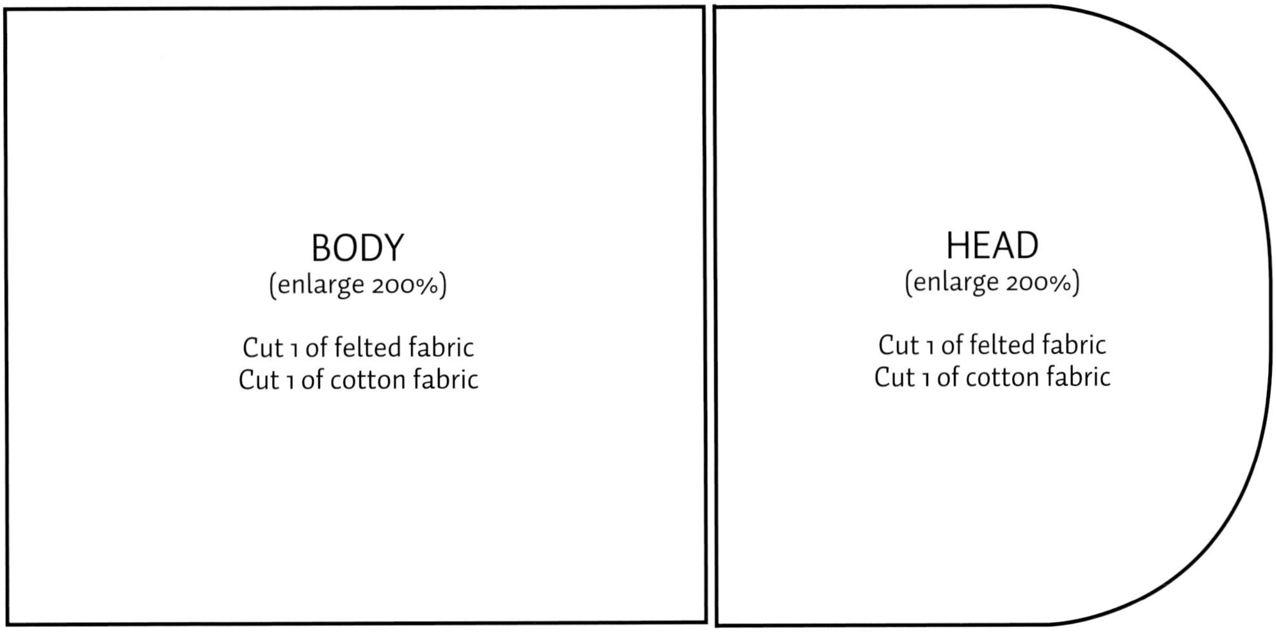
BODY
(enlarge 200%)
Cut 1 of felted fabric
Cut 1 of cotton fabric
HEAD
(enlarge 200%)
Cut 1 of felted fabric
Cut 1 of cotton fabric

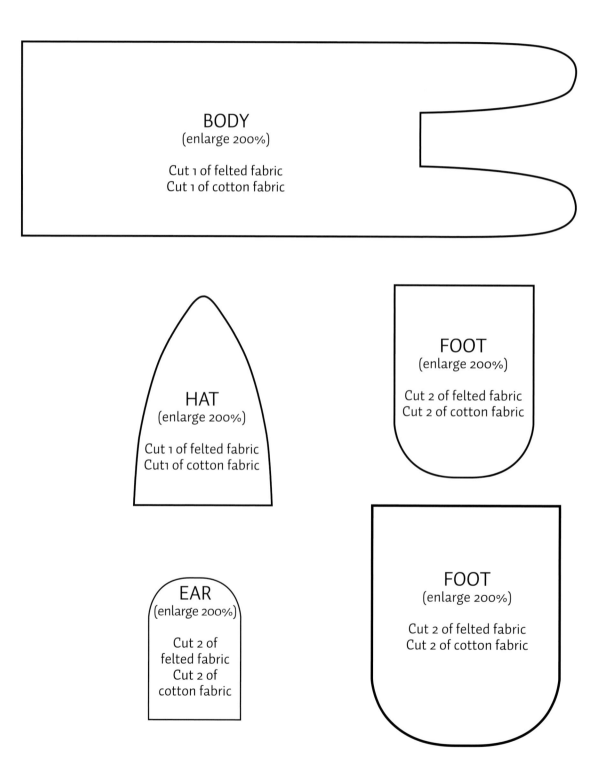

BODY
(enlarge 200%)

Cut 1 of felted fabric
Cut 1 of cotton fabric

HAT
(enlarge 200%)

Cut 1 of felted fabric
Cut1 of cotton fabric

FOOT
(enlarge 200%)

Cut 2 of felted fabric
Cut 2 of cotton fabric

EAR
(enlarge 200%)

Cut 2 of
felted fabric
Cut 2 of
cotton fabric

FOOT
(enlarge 200%)

Cut 2 of felted fabric
Cut 2 of cotton fabric

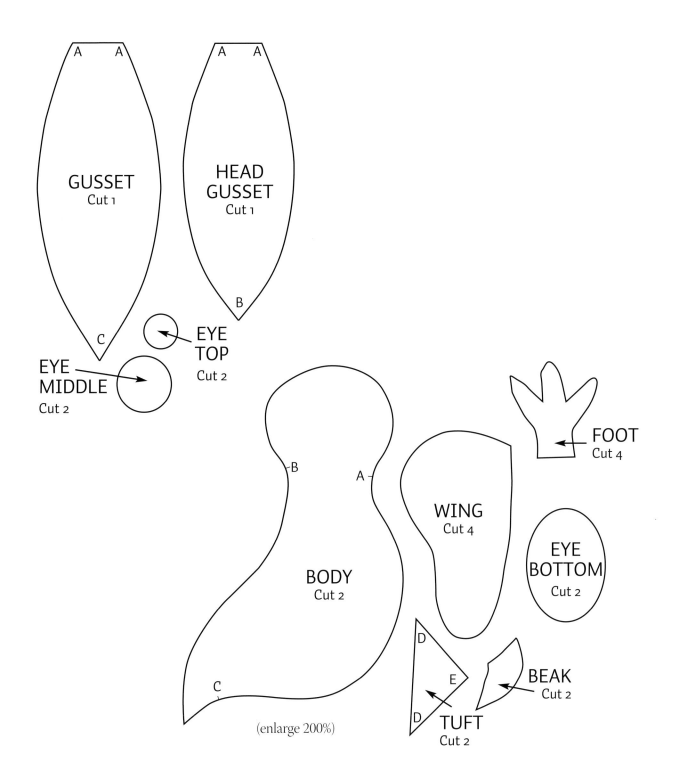

GUSSET
Cut 1

HEAD
GUSSET
Cut 1

EYE
TOP
Cut 2

EYE
MIDDLE
Cut 2

FOOT
Cut 4

BODY
Cut 2

WING
Cut 4

EYE
BOTTOM
Cut 2

BEAK
Cut 2

TUFT
Cut 2

(enlarge 200%)

Pom-pom Sweater

NOTE: Enlarge all pattern pieces (front, back, sleeve, bird) the same percentage

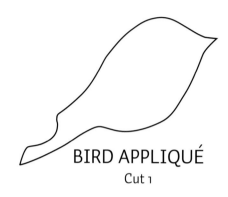

BIRD APPLIQUÉ
Cut 1

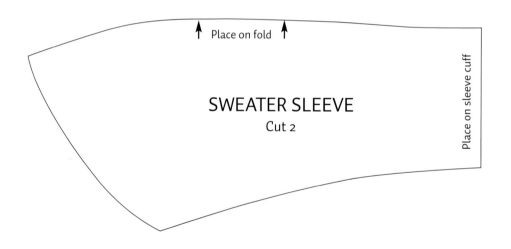

↑ Place on fold ↑

Place on sleeve cuff

SWEATER SLEEVE
Cut 2

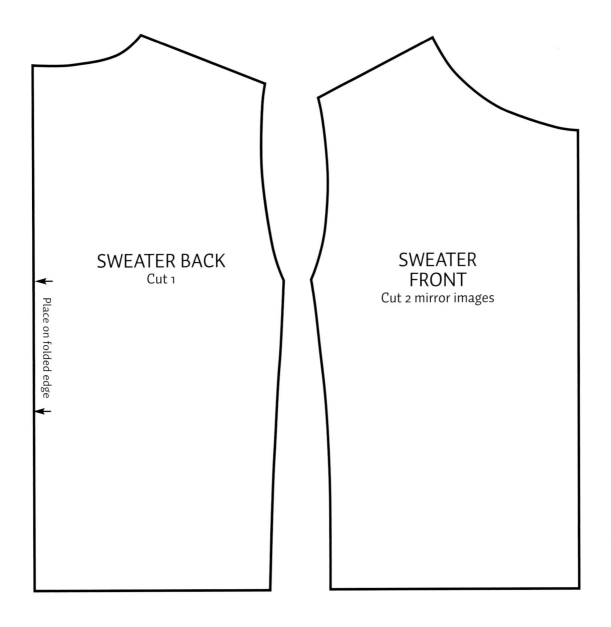

SWEATER BACK
Cut 1

Place on folded edge

SWEATER FRONT
Cut 2 mirror images

RESOURCES

Blumenthal Craft
Blumenthal-Lansing Company
http://www.buttonsplus.com

Clover
http://www.clover-usa.com/

Goodwill
http://www.goodwill.org/page/guest/about

Hancock Fabrics
http://www.hancockfabrics.com/

Jo-Ann Fabric & Crafts
www.joann.com

Michaels
The Arts & Crafts Store
www.michaels.com

Prym Consumer USA
www.dritz.com

Salvation Army
http://www.salvationarmyusa.org/usn/www_usn.nsf

CONTRIBUTORS

Susan Beal
www.susanstars.com
www.westcoastcrafty.com

Martha Bishop
www.lazygal.biz
martha@lazygal.biz

Larissa Brown
www.knitalong.net

Malka Dubrawsky
malka@stitchindye.com
www.stitchindye.com
http://stitchindye.blogspot.com (blog)
http://stitchindye.etsy.com (Etsy store)

Louise Goldsmith
Louisegtx@Yahoo.com

Tawny Holt
Armour sans Anguish
www.armoursansanguish.com
info@armoursansanguish.com

Amanda Krueger
www.abelstudio.com
www.everylittlething.typepad.com
(blog)
amanda@abelstudio.com

Anne Kuo Lukito
www.handicraftcafe.com
www.craftydiversions.com (blog)

L. K. Ludwig
The Gryphon's Feather Studio
http://gryphonsfeather.typepad.com

Jenni Pagano
www.paganodesignworks.com
Jenni@paganodesignworks.com

Mindy C. Relyea
One Wish World
www.onewishworld.com
mindy@onewishworld.com

Sarah Steedman
designer/owner
Scrappynation, LLC
www.scrappynation.com

Kim Taylor
The Sassy Crafter
www.sassycrafter.com
sassycrafter@gmail.com

About the Author

Stefanie Girard currently crafts for herself and many clients, including Plaid Enterprises, Westrim Crafts, and the Walt Disney Company.

She has written, designed, and photographed four titles for Walter Foster Publishing, on the subject of jewelry making.

She has a degree in industrial design from Pratt Institute, 1991.

Stefanie currently is senior producer of CraftTVWeekly.com and has produced other crafty shows—*Knitty Gritty, DIY Jewelry Making, Embellish This!, Sew Much More, and Simply Quilts*—for HGTV and the DIY Network

Acknowledgments

I would like to thank the Academy...
oh, sorry, wrong world. That's what happens when you live in Los Angeles!

I would like to thank my parents, Cathryn Clark Girard and Edmond Claude Girard, for genetically crafting me, then for their continued nurturing though my formative years and for sending me off to be "institutionalized" at Pratt Institute.

At Pratt, the wonderful teachers continued by teaching me "how to think"—I am truly grateful for that amazing gift. As the school motto states, "Be true to your work and your work will be true to you," which I have followed faithfully.

I would then like to thank all the fun, creative people in my life, even if they don't think of themselves as such. I am grateful for wonderful friends and family.

All the fellow creatives who have been a part of making this book: It couldn't happen without each and every one of you.

And, finally, to James Lloyd Rhodes, my beloved man, for all his patience and understanding that is required to live with a crafty gal, and all the other significant others out there who know just what I'm talking about!